WHAT YOU DO IS WHO YOU ARE

ALSO BY BEN HOROWITZ

The Hard Thing About Hard Things

WHAT
YOU DO IS
WHO
YOU ARE

HOW TO CREATE YOUR
BUSINESS CULTURE

BEN HOROWITZ

HARPER
BUSINESS

An Imprint of HarperCollinsPublishers

HarperCollins books may be purchased for educational, business, or sales promotional use. For information, please email the Special Markets Department at SPsales@harpercollins.com.

FIRST EDITION

Library of Congress Cataloging-in-Publication Data

Names: Horowitz, Ben, 1966– author.
Title: What you do is who you are / Ben Horowitz.
Description: First Edition. | New York : HarperBusiness, [2019] |
    Summary: "Keynote Straight talk and advice on building and
    running a startup from Ben Horowitz, one of Silicon Valley's most
    respected voices"— Provided by publisher.
Identifiers: LCCN 2019012403 | ISBN 9780062871336 (hardcover)
Subjects: LCSH: New business enterprises. | Corporate culture. |
    Leadership.
Classification: LCC HD62.5 .H64797 2019 | DDC 658.1/1—dc23
LC record available at https://lccn.loc.gov/2019012403

19 20 21 22 23   LSC   10 9 8 7 6 5 4 3 2 1

*This is for all the people serving time
who did what they did, but are now doing
something positive. I see what you are doing.
I know who you are.*

*One hundred percent of my portion of the
proceeds of this book will go to help people
coming out of prison change their culture
and remain free, and to the people in Haiti
trying to rebuild their society and return to
the glory of their past.*

CONTENTS

FOREWORD

Henry Louis Gates Jr.

In the secular bible that launched the Harlem Renaissance, *The New Negro: An Interpretation*, the indefatigable black bibliophile Arturo Schomburg argued in his essay "The Negro Digs Up His Past" that for too long "the Negro has been a man without a history because he has been considered a man without a worthy culture." The Puerto Rican–born Schomburg didn't just write about recovering this subsumed culture in white America; he recentered it by amassing one of history's greatest collections of manuscripts, art, and rare artifacts, which eventually provided the foundation for one of the crown jewels of the New York Public Library system: Harlem's Schomburg Center for Research in Black Culture, a fortress of learning and enlightenment located at 515 Malcolm X Boulevard in the heart of historic Harlem.

Almost a century later, another visionary in our midst, the Silicon Valley tech entrepreneur Ben Horowitz, has produced a fascinating volume at the intersection of business, leadership, and culture studies that rests on the same intellectual foundation as the mighty Schomburg. There is a lesson within a lesson at play in these pages. Instead of turning out one more book using winning case studies on the importance of fostering a thriving, mutually supportive workplace culture, Horowitz roots his own definition of innovation in the deliberate choices he makes to center the leadership stories of present, past, and long past people of color far outside the C-suite or open floor plans of today's tech giants. They include Toussaint Louverture, the genius behind the only successful slave rebellion in the history of the western hemisphere, the Haitian Revolution of the late-eighteenth/early-nineteenth century; the samurai of Japan, whose bushido code elevated virtues above values; Genghis Khan, the ultimate outsider who led one of history's most dominant armies by absorbing the best and brightest among those he defeated; and, perhaps most moving of all, James White, aka Shaka Senghor, who, on a devastating murder conviction, stepped out of quarantine into the belly of the Michigan prison system to become the leader of a violent squad called the Melanics that, over time, he shepherded toward a culture revolution focused on community uplift after prison.

By placing these dynamic figures at the center of his study, Horowitz underscores his own reputation as one of the tech industry's most philosophically committed innovators—someone who defines creation not as the execution of an already good idea but as an original one that is so cutting edge that it is considered contrarian at best. Here, Horowitz is out to persuade readers to adopt his experiential view that the most robust, sustainable cultures are those based on action, not words; an alignment of personality and strategy; an honest awareness and assessment of the norms imbibed on the first day of work by new—not veteran—employees grasping at what it will take to make it; an openness to including outside talent and perspectives; a commitment to explicit ethics and principled virtues that stand out and have meaning; and, not least, a willingness to come up with "shocking rules" within an organization that indelibly and inescapably prompt others to ask, "Why?"

To prove "why" himself, Horowitz doesn't go to the usual well of Fortune 500 winners but to the outer edges of history, where we discover leaders whose stories reveal lessons and insights that are actually core to the creation of culture itself.

In its essence, *What You Do Is Who You Are* is a book whose content and structure—including the epigraphs Horowitz invokes from the canon of hip-hop legends—perfectly reflect the thesis at work in its pages. It also happens to be an energetic read, with surprising and illuminating applications of the lessons of Louverture, Senghor, and company to the contemporary business and political scene that Horowitz himself, as the former CEO of LoudCloud and cofounder of Andreessen Horowitz, inhabits as one of today's most uniquely gifted leaders. In this way, Horowitz calls upon a key aspect of the African-American tradition of "signifying"—riffing as a mode of homage, a nod of admiration and respect—and he does so with penetrating insight and memorable effect. The book is also an inspiring nod to an historical tradition that intellectual antecedents such as Arturo Schomburg—caught in the throes of Jim Crow segregated America—sacrificed so much to canonize, hoping that generations hence would see "behind the veil," as W.E.B. Du Bois put it, to mine lessons for a new, truly cosmopolitan world culture in which they could only dream of flourishing. By centering his transformational volume on culture-makers whose wisdom is found on the margins, Horowitz gives us an instant classic with the potential to redefine "what we do" and, thereby, "who we are."

WHAT YOU DO IS WHO YOU ARE

INTRODUCTION: WHAT YOU DO IS WHO YOU ARE

> Revel in being discarded, or having all your energies
> exhausted in vain; only those who have endured
> hardship will be of use. Samurai who have never
> erred before will never have what it takes.
> —*Hagakure*

When I first founded a company, one called LoudCloud, I sought advice from CEOs and industry leaders. They all told me, "Pay attention to your culture. Culture is the most important thing."

But when I asked these leaders, "What exactly is culture, and how can I affect mine?" they became extremely vague. I spent the next eighteen years trying to figure this question out. Is culture dogs at work and yoga in the break room? No, those are perks. Is it your corporate values? No, those are aspirations. Is it the personality and priorities of the CEO? That helps shape the culture, but it is far from the thing itself.

When I was the CEO of LoudCloud, I figured that our company culture would be just a reflection of my values, behaviors, and personality. So I focused all my energy on "leading by example." To my bewilderment and horror, that method did not scale as the company grew and diversified. Our culture became a hodgepodge of different cultures fostered under different managers, and most of these cultures were unintentional. Some managers were screamers who intimidated their people, others neglected to give any feedback, some didn't bother returning emails—it was a big mess.

I had a middle manager—I'll call him Thorston—who I thought was pretty good. He worked in marketing and was a great storyteller (an essential marketing skill). I was shocked to find out, from overhearing casual conversations, that he was taking storytelling to another level by constantly lying about everything. Thorston was soon working elsewhere, but I knew I had to deal with a much deeper problem: because it had taken me years to find out that he was a compulsive liar, during which time he'd been promoted, it had become culturally okay to lie at LoudCloud. The object lesson had been learned. It did not matter that I never endorsed it: his getting away with it made it seem okay. How could I undo that lesson and restore our culture? I hadn't the first clue.

To really understand how this stuff works, I knew I had to dig deeper. So I asked myself, How many of the following questions can be resolved by turning to your corporate goals or mission statement?

- Is that phone call so important I need to return it today, or can it wait till tomorrow?
- Can I ask for a raise before my annual review?
- Is the quality of this document good enough or should I keep working on it?

- Do I have to be on time for that meeting?
- Should I stay at the Four Seasons or the Red Roof Inn?
- When I negotiate this contract, what's more important: the price or the partnership?
- Should I point out what my peers do wrong, or what they do right?
- Should I go home at 5 p.m. or 8 p.m.?
- How hard do I need to study the competition?
- Should we discuss the color of this new product for five minutes or thirty hours?
- If I know something is badly broken in the company, should I say something? Whom should I tell?
- Is winning more important than ethics?

The answer is zero.

There aren't any "right answers" to those questions. The right answers for your company depend on what your company is, what it does, and what it wants to be. In fact, how your employees answer these kinds of questions *is* your culture. Because your culture is how your company makes decisions when you're not there. It's the set of assumptions your employees use to resolve the problems they face every day. It's how they behave when no one is looking. If you don't methodically set your culture, then two-thirds of it will end up being accidental, and the rest will be a mistake.

So how do you design and shape these nearly invisible behaviors? I asked that of Shaka Senghor, who ran a powerful gang in the Michigan prison system in the 1990s and 2000s. Senghor knew that the lives of his guys depended on the gang's culture. He told me, "It's complex. Say someone steals one of your guys' toothbrushes, what do you do?"

I said, "That seems innocent enough. Maybe the thief just wanted clean teeth?"

He corrected me: "A guy doesn't take that risk for clean teeth. It's a diagnostic. If we don't respond, then he knows he can rob your guy of something larger or rape him or kill him and take over his business. So if I do nothing, I put all our members at risk. Killing the guy would be a big deterrent—but it would also create a superviolent culture." He spread his hands. "As I said, it's complex."

Identifying the culture you want is hard: you have to figure out not only where your company is trying to go, but the road it should take to get there. For many startups, a culture of frugality is vital, so it makes sense to require that employees stay at the Red Roof Inn. But if Google is paying a salesperson $500,000 a year and it wants to retain her, it will probably prefer that she sleep well at the Four Seasons before her big meeting with Procter & Gamble.

Likewise, long days are standard in the startup world— you're in a race against time. But at Slack, CEO Stewart Butterfield is convinced that if you actually work hard when you are at work, you can efficiently get a lot done. He punches out early and encourages his employees to do the same.

The culture that works for Apple would never work for Amazon. At Apple, generating the most brilliant designs in the world is paramount. To reinforce that message, it spent $5 billion on its sleek new headquarters. At Amazon, Jeff Bezos famously said, "Your fat margins are my opportunity." To reinforce that message, he made the company be frugal in everything, down to his employees' ten-dollar desks. Both cultures work. Apple designs dramatically more beautiful products than Amazon, while Amazon's products are dramatically cheaper than Apple's.

Culture is not like a mission statement; you can't just set it up and have it last forever. There's a saying in the military that if you see something below standard and do nothing, then you've set a new standard. This is also true of culture—if you see something off-culture and ignore it, you've created a new culture. Meanwhile, as business conditions shift and your strategy evolves, you have to keep changing your culture accordingly. The target is always moving.

CULTURE IS THE STRONG FORCE

In business, if you have a strong culture but a product nobody wants, you fail. So culture might appear to be weaker than product. But if you look more deeply, over time, culture can overcome the seemingly invincible structural barriers of an era and transform the behavior of entire industries and social systems. From this broader perspective, culture is the strong force in the universe.

In the 1970s, a bunch of poor kids from the Bronx created a new art form, hip-hop. In a single generation they overcame poverty, racism, and massive opposition from the music industry to build the world's most popular musical genre. They changed global culture by inventing a culture premised on candor and a hustler's mentality.

The hustler's mentality could be seen in how hip-hop DJs sourced their basic building block: breakbeats. Breakbeats were the part of the song that everyone got excited about on the dance floor—the beat-heavy breakdown sections that featured drums and bass, or just drums. The freshest breakbeats, the ones people hadn't heard before, were often found on obscure records. Because these records were obscure, the record companies wouldn't restock them if they suddenly sold out, which created a supply-chain problem. Hip-hop's entrepreneurial culture worked right around it. Ralph McDaniels, who put the first rap videos on television and who coined the term "shout-out," told me:

> A guy named Lenny Roberts supplied these records to the stores and he knew precisely what was going to sell, because he was from the Bronx and that's where it was all breaking. He marketed these breakbeats by giving them to Afrika Bambaataa or Grandmaster Flash, and when Flash played it every DJ would go, "Oh, I've got to have that record," and the records would instantly sell out. So Lenny pressed his own records with just the breakbeats: the Breakbeats Volume One, Breakbeats Volume Two, etc. He didn't have the rights, of course, but nobody was paying any attention.

People often ask me why I preface much of what I write with quotes from hip-hop. In part it's a hangover from my failed career as a rapper—true story. But mostly it's because the majority of my ideas about entrepreneurship, business, and culture occur to me while I'm listening to hip-hop, so it's my way of giving credit where credit is due. I always felt that early hip-hop songs like Eric B. & Rakim's "Follow the Leader" or Run-DMC's "King of Rock" were about what I was doing as an entrepreneur. They are the culture in which I work.

While the hustling part of hip-hop culture made the business go, it was the honesty that drew the fans. The great rapper Nas told me that as a kid:

> The rawness was what I gravitated towards. The world was supposed to be this picture-perfect place, the Brady Bunch. We're all trying to be the Brady Bunch, but really we're the Little Rascals. Rap explained what's really going on—the crimes, the poverty, the corrupt police. Rap cleansed itself of pimp-sounding music or gospel-sounding music or a funky sound or a hippie sound. It extracted all that other stuff out of it and ripped itself raw until it was simply about honesty.

A continent away from the Bronx, a group of engineers in California established a set of cultural innovations that would end up changing how almost every business operates. In the 1960s, Bob Noyce, the co-inventor of the integrated circuit, or microchip, ran

Fairchild Semiconductor, a unit of Fairchild Camera and Instrument Corporation.

Fairchild Camera, based in New York City, did business the east coast way, which had become the way big businesses across the country conducted themselves. Fairchild's owner, Sherman Fairchild, lived in a glass-and-marble town house in Manhattan. His top executives got cars and drivers and reserved parking places. As Tom Wolfe observed in his 1983 *Esquire* story "The Tinkerings of Robert Noyce," "Corporations in the East adopted a feudal approach to organization, without even being aware of it. There were kings and lords, and there were vassals, soldiers, yeomen, and serfs."

Bob Noyce didn't believe any of that made sense when it was his individual engineers—the yeomen—who were inventing products and driving the business. So Fairchild Semiconductor did things differently. Everyone was expected at work by 8 a.m., and whoever got in first got the best parking space. The company's building in San Jose was a warehouse filled with cubicles, and nobody wore a suit.

Noyce didn't hire professional managers. He said, "Coaching, and not direction, is the first quality of leadership now. Get the barriers out of the way to let people do the things they do well." This created a new culture, a culture of empowerment: everyone was in charge and Noyce was there to help. If a researcher had an idea, he could pursue it for a year before anyone would start inquiring about results.

Employees who got a taste of Noyce's culture of independence split off to start their own companies, including Raytheon Semiconductor, Signetics, General Microelectronics, Intersil, Advanced Micro Devices (AMD), and Qualidyne. Without exactly meaning to, Noyce had created the culture of Silicon Valley.

In 1968, Noyce himself split off to start a new company, resigning from Fairchild Semiconductor after being passed over for CEO of Fairchild Camera. He and his colleague Gordon Moore—the coiner of Moore's law, which holds that microchip capacity doubles every eighteen months while its price falls in half—and a young physicist named Andy Grove founded Intel to tackle the nascent field of data storage.

At Intel, Noyce took his egalitarian ideas to a new level. Everyone worked in one big room with partitions separating them; Noyce himself sat at a secondhand metal desk. Lunch was deli sandwiches and soda. There was no layer of vice presidents; Noyce and Moore oversaw business segments run by middle managers who had enormous decision-making power. In meetings, the leader set the agenda, but everyone else was equal.

And, crucially, Noyce gave the engineers and most of the office workers substantial stock options. He believed that in a business driven by research and products, the engineers would behave more like owners if they actually owned the company.

Wolfe observed that "At Intel everyone—Noyce included—was expected to attend sessions on 'the Intel Culture.'" The culture was drilled into new employees by Andy Grove (who would go on to become the company's CEO and a famous cultural innovator). Grove would ask, "How would you sum up the Intel approach?" Someone might answer, "At Intel you don't wait for someone else to do it. You take the ball yourself and run with it." Grove would reply, "Wrong. At Intel you take the ball yourself and you let the air out and you fold the ball up and put it in your pocket. Then you take another ball and run with it and when you've crossed the goal you take the second ball out of your pocket and reinflate it and score twelve points instead of six."

This atmosphere allowed ideas to prosper; if Silicon Valley is about anything, it's about the primacy of the idea. Breakthrough ideas have traditionally been difficult to manage for two reasons: 1) innovative ideas fail far more than they succeed, and 2) innovative ideas are always controversial before they succeed. If everyone could instantly understand them, they wouldn't be innovative.

Imagine a culture of strict accountability that punishes failure—a very common culture back east, where executives strove to maintain their status, and failure was to be avoided at all costs. Now consider an idea that has a 90 percent chance of failing, but that would pay off at 1,000 to 1. Despite it being an extraordinarily good bet, the company that punishes failure will never fund it.

Hierarchies are good at weeding out obviously bad ideas. By the time an idea makes it all the way up the chain, it will have been compared to all the other ideas in the system, with the obviously good ideas ranked at the top. This seems like common sense. The problem is that obviously good ideas are not truly innovative, and truly innovative ideas often look like very bad ideas when they're introduced. Western Union famously passed on the opportunity to buy Alexander Graham Bell's patents and technology for the telephone. At the time, phone calls were extremely noisy and easy to misinterpret, and they couldn't span long distances, and Western Union knew from its telegram business that profitable communication depended on accuracy and widespread reach. And Wikipedia was considered a joke when it started. How could something written by a crowd replace the work of the world's top scholars? Today it is so much more comprehensive than anything that came before it that it's widely considered the only encyclopedia.

The Intel culture, by elevating the individual and giving breakthrough ideas a chance, inaugurated a better way to do business. My business partner Marc Andreessen wrote an essay a few years ago called "Software Is Eating the World." He described how technology has spread beyond the technology industry to take over every traditional business, from bookstores to taxi fleets to hotels. Existing companies have been forced to adopt aspects of Noyce's culture or else expose themselves to an onslaught of existential threats. We've seen General Motors adopt stock options as it moved into autonomous vehicles by buying Cruise Automation, and Walmart employ a similar approach with its purchase of Jet.com.

Since tech became a consumer phenomenon, thousands of nontech people have come up with great ideas that use technology. But if their startups outsource their engineering, they almost always fail. Why? It turns out that it's easy to build an app or a website that meets the specification of some initial idea, but far more difficult to build something that will scale, evolve, handle edge cases gracefully, etc. A great engineer will only invest the time and effort to do all those things, to build a product that will grow with the company, if she has ownership in the company—literally as well as figuratively. Bob Noyce understood that, created the culture to support it, and changed the world.

WHAT MAKES A CULTURE WORK?

Culture clearly has a powerful effect. So how do you shape it, how do you set it deep in people's minds, and how do you fix it when it goes wrong?

These questions led me to larger questions and a wider frame of reference. How does culture work in a variety of different contexts? What makes it last for more than a few years?

I have long been interested in history, and particularly in how people behaved differently from what I would have expected, given the circumstances they were born into. For instance, I would never have expected that a man who was born into slavery and who would one day free the slaves of Haiti would own slaves himself along the way—but he did. Understanding how historical cultures shaped people's views led me to begin considering what they had to do to change themselves and their culture. Grasping that seemed to be the key to creating the kind of culture that I wanted.

I selected four models in particular, one of whom is still very much alive. I wasn't looking for ideal cultural end states—some of the models produced extremely violent or otherwise problematic cultures—but for people who were outstandingly effective in getting the cultures they wanted. Each of these models made me ask giant questions:

- Why has there been only one successful slave revolt in human history? And how did Haiti's Toussaint Louverture reprogram slave culture to orchestrate it?

- How did bushido, the code of the samurai, enable the warrior class to rule Japan for seven hundred years and shape modern Japanese culture? What set of cultural virtues empowered them? The samurai called their principles "virtues" rather than "values"; virtues are what you *do*, while values are merely what you believe. As we'll see, doing is what matters. (In what follows I will use "virtues" to refer to the ideal, and "values" to refer to what most companies now espouse.) How exactly did the samurai focus their culture on actions?

- How did Genghis Khan build the world's largest empire? He was a total outsider, imprisoned as a youngster by his own tiny nomadic tribe. It's easy to see how that made him want to smash existing hierarchies. But how, exactly, was he able to create an innovative and inclusive meritocracy? One that enabled him to constantly grow and improve while his foes were standing still?

- How did Shaka Senghor, sentenced to nineteen years in a Michigan prison for murder, make his prison gang the tightest, most ferocious group in the yard—and then transform it into something else entirely? How did culture turn him into a killer? How did he rise to dominate that culture? How did he take a group of outcasts and turn them into a cohesive team? Finally, how did he recognize what he disliked about his regime, and, by changing himself, change the entire prison culture?

Companies—just like gangs, armies, and nations—are large organizations that rise or fall because of the daily microbehaviors of the human beings that compose them. But figuring out whether the root cause of a company's success is its culture or some other factor isn't easy. Most business books don't look at culture from a wider, more sociological perspective. And most attempt to dissect successful companies' cultures after the companies have succeeded. This approach confuses cause and effect. There are plenty of massively successful companies with weak, inconsistent, or even toxic cultures; a desirable product can overcome a miserable environment, at least for a while. If you don't believe me, read up on Enron.

To avoid survivorship bias—the logical error of concentrating on companies that succeeded and falsely concluding that it was their culture that made them great—I try not to reverse engineer. Instead I look at the cultural techniques that leaders used as they tried to strengthen their culture in specific ways, and show how those efforts played out. So you won't find any absolute "best cultures" in this book, just techniques to make your own culture do what you want it to.

HOW TO READ THIS BOOK

I start by examining the four historical models described earlier, and then break out modern-day examples of those same cultural techniques. As you read these first seven chapters, think about how leaders like Toussaint Louverture and Genghis Khan saw culture, and the tools they devised to shift it even under extremely difficult circumstances, when everything seemed to be conspiring against them. Take note of practices you might want to emulate, and how perspectives well outside your own might be surprisingly pertinent. How did the samurai design a culture whose elements all fit neatly together? How is Shaka Senghor's experience, coming into prison as a young man and having to figure out how it worked, relevant to new employees at your company?

Creating a culture is more complex than just trying to get your people to behave the way you want them to when no one is looking. Remember that your employees are far from uniform. They come from different countries, races, genders, backgrounds, even eras. Each one brings to your organization a different cultural point of departure. To get all of them to conform to and be reasonably happy with a common set of norms is a challenging puzzle.

To get them to be who you want, you will first need

to see them for who they are. I wish I could give you a simple set of steps to do that, but there is no formula. Instead we'll consider all these questions from a variety of perspectives. To that end, these chapters also feature modern-day case studies, usually worked up from my conversations with leaders who tried to change their companies. For instance, I examine how Toussaint Louverture's cultural techniques were applied—or should have been applied—by Reed Hastings at Netflix, Travis Kalanick at Uber, and Hillary Clinton, and how Genghis Khan's vision of cultural inclusiveness has parallels in the work of Don Thompson, the first African-American CEO of McDonald's, and of Maggie Wilderotter, the CEO who led Frontier Communications.

I begin the second part of the book by walking you through how to understand your own personality and your company's strategy and how to use that understanding to build the culture you need to succeed. Culture only works if the leader visibly participates in and vocally champions it. But most people don't walk around with a supersharp definition of their personal cultural values. So how do you identify who you are and what parts of you belong in the organization (and don't belong)? How do you become the kind of leader that you yourself want to follow?

Then I look at edge cases that can place your culture in conflict with itself or with your business priorities. And finally, I discuss a few components that probably belong in every culture, and give you a checklist of crucial principles.

Culture isn't a magical set of rules that makes everyone behave the way you'd like. It's a system of behaviors that you hope most people will follow, most of the time. Critics love to attack companies for having a "broken culture" or being "morally corrupt," but it's actually a minor miracle if a culture isn't dysfunctional. No large organization ever gets anywhere near 100 percent compliance on every value, but some do much better than others. Our aim here is to be better, not perfect.

As a final word of discouragement: a great culture does not get you a great company. If your product isn't superior or the market doesn't want it, your company will fail no matter how good its culture is. Culture is to a company as nutrition and training are to an aspiring professional athlete. If the athlete is talented enough, he'll succeed despite relatively poor nutrition and a below-average training regimen. If he lacks talent, perfect nutrition and relentless training will not qualify him for the Olympics. But great nutrition and training make every athlete better.

If a great culture won't ensure success, why bother? In the end, the people who work for you won't remember the press releases or the awards. They'll lose track of the quarterly ups and downs. They may even grow hazy about the products. But they will never forget how it felt to work there, or the kind of people they became as a result. The company's character and ethos will be the one thing they carry with them. It will be the glue that holds them together when things go wrong. It will be their guide to the tiny, daily decisions they make that add up to a sense of genuine purpose.

This book is not a comprehensive set of techniques for creating a perfect culture. There is no one ideal. A culture's strengths may also be its weaknesses. And sometimes you have to break a core principle of your culture to survive. Culture is crucial, but if the company fails because you insist on cultural purity, you're doing it wrong.

Instead, the book will take you on a journey through culture, from ancient to modern. Along the way, you will learn how to answer a question fundamental to any organization: who are we? A simple-seeming question that's not simple at all. Because who you are is how people talk about you when you're not around. How do you treat your customers? Are you there for people in a pinch? Can you be trusted?

Who you are is not the values you list on the wall. It's not what you say at an all-hands. It's not your marketing campaign. It's not even what you believe.

It's what you do. What you do is who you are. This book aims to help you do the things you need to do so you can be who you want to be.

I CULTURE AND REVOLUTION: THE STORY OF TOUSSAINT LOUVERTURE

Blood of a slave, heart of a king.
—*Nas*

After I sold my company Opsware to Hewlett-Packard in 2007 and helped with the transition, I had nothing to do. As an entrepreneur, I had trained myself to think in contrarian ways. The secret to finding a breakthrough idea, as Peter Thiel says, is that you have to believe something that nobody else does. So I started thinking about ideas that everyone believes. The first that came to mind was "Slavery was so incredibly horrible that it's almost unimaginable that it existed at such scale." What was the contrarian point of view?

What if it were more shocking that slavery ever ended?

As absurd as that sounded, once I dug into the matter, I felt like I might be onto something. Slavery had been around since the beginning of recorded history. It was endorsed by all the major religions; long and detailed sections of the Bible and the Koran are dedicated to it. In the 1600s, more than half of the world's population was enslaved. How did it ever end? The stamping out of slavery is one of humanity's great stories. And the best story within that story is the Haitian Revolution.

In our long history, there has been only one successful slave revolution that led to an independent state. There were surely uprisings by the slaves of the Han Dynasty and the Christian slaves of the Ottoman Empire, and there are numerous accounts of rebellions by some of the ten million Africans held in bondage during the slave trade that thrived from the fifteenth to the nineteenth centuries. But only one revolt succeeded. Certainly, strong motivation fueled every attempt—there is no more inspiring cause than freedom. So why only one victory?

Slavery chokes the development of culture by dehumanizing its subjects, and broken cultures don't win wars. As a slave, none of your work accrues to you. You have no reason to care about doing things thoughtfully and systematically when you and your family members can be sold or killed at any moment. To keep you from learning about other ways of life, communicating with other slaves, or knowing what your masters are up to, you are forbidden to learn to read and have no ready tools for accumulating and storing knowledge. You can be raped, whipped, or dismembered at your captor's pleasure. This constellation of atrocities leads to a culture with low levels of education and trust and a short-term focus on survival—none of which help in building a cohesive fighting force.

So how did one man, born a slave, reprogram slave culture? How did Toussaint Louverture build an army of slaves in Saint-Domingue (the prerevolutionary name of Haiti) into a fighting force so fearsome it defeated Spain, Britain, and France—the greatest military forces in Europe? How did this slave army inflict more casualties on Napoleon than he would suffer at Waterloo?

You might suspect that slavery was less brutal in Saint-Domingue than elsewhere. Did Louverture have a particularly easy go of it?

Nope. During the slave-trade era, fewer than 500,000 slaves were brought to the United States, while about 900,000 were introduced to Saint-Domingue. Yet by 1789, the United States contained nearly 700,000 slaves and Saint-Domingue just 465,000. In other words, the death rate on Saint-Domingue overwhelmed the birth rate. The island was a slaughterhouse.

Slaves in Saint-Domingue were treated with almost incomprehensible brutality. C. L. R. James describes it in his masterpiece, *The Black Jacobins*:

> *Whipping was interrupted in order to pass a piece of hot wood on the buttocks of the victim; salt, pepper, citron, cinders, aloes, and hot ashes were poured on the bleeding wounds. Mutilations were common, limbs, ears and sometimes the private parts, to deprive them of the pleasures which they could indulge in without*

expense. Their masters poured burning wax on their arms and hands and shoulders, emptied the boiling cane sugar over their heads, burned them alive, roasted them on slow fires, filled them with gunpowder and blew them up with a match; buried them up to the neck and smeared their heads with sugar that the flies might devour them.

This torturous environment led to a predictably abject and suspicious culture. Black slaves and mulattoes hated each other. The man of color who was nearly white despised the man of color who was half white, who in turn despised the man of color who was a quarter white, and so on.

What's more, the military power poised to crush any rebellion was enormous. Saint-Domingue provided a third of the world's sugar and half of its coffee; it was the most profitable colony in the world, and therefore of massive strategic interest. Every empire wanted to control it.

So no, this environment was not ideal for rebellion.

Louverture's rebellion was no mere slave revolt, but a much more complex disruption premised on meticulous military strategy and aimed at lasting change. Considered a genius even by his enemies, Louverture was able to blend the best, most useful elements from slave culture and from the colonial European culture that had enslaved him—and to mix in his own brilliant cultural insights. The resulting hybrid culture inspired a ferocious army, a cunning diplomacy, and a farsighted perspective on economics and governance.

WHO WAS TOUSSAINT LOUVERTURE?

Louverture was born into slavery on the Bréda estate sugar plantation in Saint-Domingue in, we think, 1743. Much of his personal history is fragmentary and uncertain—no one bothered to keep detailed records about obscure slaves. Historians also disagree about many of the turning points in the country's revolution, agreeing only that its leader was an extraordinary man.

As a child, Louverture was so frail his parents called him "Sickly Stick" and did not expect him to live. Yet by age twelve, he had surpassed all the boys on the plantation with his athletic feats. In time he became known as the colony's greatest horseman. Even as he neared sixty, he often rode 125 miles in a day.

Louverture was just five feet two and by no means handsome. Laconic, with a stern, probing glance, he was immensely energetic and focused. He slept two hours a night and could live for days on a few bananas and a glass of water. His education, position, and character gave him tremendous prestige among his fellow slaves long before the revolution. He never doubted that his destiny was to be their leader.

While still a teenager, he was made caretaker of the estate's mules and oxen—a post usually held by a white man. Louverture seized this rare opportunity to educate himself in his free time and to read through his master's library, including Julius Caesar's *Commentaries* and Abbé Raynal's *Histoire des deux Indes,* or History of two Indies, an encyclopedic account of trade between Europe and the Far East. Caesar's work helped him understand politics and the art of war, and Raynal's gave him a thorough grounding in the economics of the region and of Europe.

But his education and position did not exempt him from the fundamental indignity of being black. One day, as he was returning from Mass carrying his prayer book, a white man took notice. Louverture would recall that the man "broke my head with a wooden stick while telling me 'do you not know that a negro should not read?'" Louverture apologized and stumbled home. He kept the vest soaked with his blood as a reminder of the incident. Years later, after the rebellion began, he met his tormenter again and, his biographer Philippe Girard writes with satisfaction, "killed him on the spot."

The estate's attorney, François Bayon de Libertat, recognized Louverture's abilities and made him coachman. Around 1776, he freed Louverture; Louverture was now paid to drive Libertat's coach. At the time, fewer than one in a thousand black men were set free. The father of the Haitian Revolution earned his freedom by forming a special bond with a white man.

Louverture used every carriage ride with Libertat to expand his network, making contact with nearly all of his future allies. The rides also enabled him first to understand, and then to master, French colonial ways. Louverture gradually came to a realization that no one else in colonial Saint-Domingue had arrived at: culture, not color, determined behavior.

One astonishing demonstration of this truth was that

after he'd been freed, Louverture purchased slaves, usually to free them in turn. But he also strove to get ahead in the colonial manner, the only manner available to him at that point: off of slave labor. In 1779, in a brief and unsuccessful attempt to make money, he leased a coffee plantation worked by thirteen slaves. One of them was Jean-Jacques Dessalines, who in later years would become his second in command—and then go on to betray him.

If there was a motivational trigger for Louverture to turn from commerce to statecraft, perhaps it came in 1784, when he read a famous passage written by Abbé Raynal, a proponent of liberty who hoped for a slave revolt: "A courageous chief only is wanted. Where is he, that great man whom Nature owes to her vexed, oppressed, and tormented children? Where is he?" According to one account, Louverture read this passage over and over, dreaming that he might be that courageous chief.

LOUVERTURE'S RISE

Once news of the French Revolution of 1789 reached the island, insurrection was in the air. The initial rebellion on the Manquets plantation in 1791 stirred up slaves on the surrounding plantations, and within a few years the insurrectionary force grew to fifty thousand men, one hundred times the size of the largest slave revolt in U.S. history.

Louverture had known of and perhaps helped shape plans for the uprising, but he waited to see how it would go, only joining in a month after it began. The colony's political situation was extremely complicated, with numerous factions, parties, and shifting alliances, and it was unclear what would happen on your plantation next week, let alone to the whole island over time.

When Louverture joined the rebels he was about forty-seven and already known as "Old Toussaint." Within a few months he had appointed himself brigadier general and was leading one of the three chief rebel groups. To build support, Louverture implied that he was acting on behalf of the French king, Louis XVI, who, he said, had issued him a document promising the rebels three days of rest a week in exchange for their efforts. He was able to pull off this ruse because almost none of his followers could read and write.

Between 1791 and 1793, he and the rebels made such progress that France dispatched eleven thousand troops to hold them back—more than the nation sent abroad during the U.S. War of Independence.

After Louis XVI was guillotined in Paris in 1793, the British and Spanish invaded Saint-Domingue, each hoping to seize the prize while France was preoccupied. Once Spain declared war on France, Louverture went to the Spanish commander and offered to integrate his six hundred men into the Spanish army, which other rebellious slave groups were also joining. And so Louverture became a colonel in the Spanish army, fighting the French.

The following year, seeing an advantage for himself and his troops, Louverture defected to the French army. Within a year, he and his men, now five thousand strong, had retaken almost all of the French towns he had just conquered for Spain, and subdued several rebel groups still allied with the Spanish. These victories, in concert with military setbacks in Europe, forced Spain to sue for peace. Louverture had defeated his first European superpower.

Next he faced the British, who had sent two large battalions to Saint-Domingue. Unprepared to tackle a large professional army, Louverture began retreating in 1795 and maintained a defensive posture for two years, even as the remaining blacks on the island, some 500,000 men in all, joined his side. Time, guerrilla skirmishing, and yellow fever wore down Louverture's foes. Twelve thousand of the twenty thousand British soldiers who arrived on the island were buried there, and in 1798 Louverture negotiated the departure of their remaining forces. He had defeated his second European superpower.

In 1801 he invaded Santo Domingo, the Spanish part of the island that is now the Dominican Republic, and defeated the Spanish for good. On July 7, 1801, he became governor of the entire island where he had once been a slave. He promptly published a new constitution. Saint-Domingue would still be a French colony, in name, but the constitution abolished slavery, opened all jobs to all races, and made the territory functionally independent. In just ten years Louverture and his army had accomplished the unimaginable.

HOW LOUVERTURE REPROGRAMMED SLAVE CULTURE

In 1797, in the midst of the long revolt, Louverture demonstrated that he could not only lead troops, but also persuade and inspire civilians with his vision for a new way of life. Vincent de Vaublanc, a white deputy from Saint-Domingue, warned the French Parliament that the colony had fallen under the control of "ignorant and brutish negroes." Vaublanc's speech had a tremendous impact, and there were rumors of a counterrevolution being plotted in Paris.

Louverture's response was to publish a justification of the Haitian Revolution that laid out his theory of race and culture. As Philippe Girard wrote, "One by one he listed Vaublanc's accusations; one by one he took them apart. Blacks were not lazy and ignorant savages: slavery had made them so. Some violence had indeed taken place in the Haitian Revolution, but violence had also taken place in the French Revolution, he reminded his readers; the slaves had in fact proved remarkably merciful toward the planters who had so cruelly oppressed them." Louverture demonstrated that these former slaves had elevated their culture to a point where he could in justice close the letter by reaffirming black freedmen's "right to be called French Citizens."

In 1798, after Louverture negotiated peace and a diplomatic relationship with the British, the *London Gazette* wrote:

> *Toussaint L'Ouverture is a negro and in the jargon of war has been called a brigand. But according to all ac-*

counts, he is a negro born to vindicate the claims of this species and to show that the character of men is independent of exterior color.

This newspaper, in a nation that traded more African slaves than any other, published that encomium thirty-five years before Britain abolished slavery. As Louverture had envisioned, Europeans were beginning to see that it was the culture of slavery rather than the nature of the slaves themselves that shaped their behavior.

Some Americans began to see it that way, too. In 1798, during a rift with France, the U.S. Congress banned all trade with France and its colonies. Commerce to and from Saint-Domingue came to a standstill. Louverture sent a man named Joseph Bunel to see the U.S. secretary of state, Thomas Pickering, about lifting the embargo. Louverture shrewdly selected a white man as his ambassador to appeal to the sensibilities of the slave-owning country. It worked. In 1799, the U.S. Congress authorized President John Adams to exempt from the trade embargo any French territory that did not interfere with American trade. The law was so transparently intended for Saint-Domingue that it was nicknamed "the Louverture clause."

Pickering wrote Louverture to let him know that the United States would resume commerce with Saint-Domingue. Philippe Girard characterizes the letter beautifully in his masterpiece, *Toussaint Louverture*:

He closed with an arresting flourish: "I am with due considerations, Sir, your obedient servant." To a former slave, the niceties of diplomatic language must have had a peculiar ring: Louverture was not used to hearing prominent white men refer to themselves as his "obedient servant."

More than sixty-five years before the Thirteenth Amendment ended slavery in the United States, Congress made special provisions for a black man. They negotiated with him not through the lens of the color of his skin but through the lens of the culture he had created.

Louverture used seven key tactics, which I examine below, to transform slave culture into one respected around the world. You can use them to change any organization's culture.

Keep What Works

To create his army, Louverture began with five hundred handpicked men who learned the art of war with him as he drilled and trained them assiduously. In this way, he was able to create the new culture with minimal divergence. He knew he had to elevate his fighters' culture to make the army effective, but he also knew that his slave culture had great strengths and that creating a new civilization out of whole cloth—as Lenin would later try and fail to do—would never succeed. People don't easily adopt new cultural norms and they simply can't absorb an entirely new system all at once.

He used two preexisting cultural strengths to great effect. The first was the songs the slaves sang at their midnight celebrations of voodoo. Louverture was a devout

Catholic who would later outlaw voodoo—but he was also a pragmatist who used the tools at hand. So he converted this simple, memorable vocal template into an advanced communications technology. The Europeans had no means of long-distance, encrypted communication, but his army did. His soldiers would place themselves in the woods surrounding the enemy, scattered in clumps. They would begin their voodoo songs—which were incomprehensible to the European troops—and when they reached a certain verse, it was the signal to attack in concert.

Second, many of Louverture's soldiers brought military skills with them. Among his warriors were veterans of wars on the Angola-Congo coast. Louverture applied their guerrilla tactics, particularly their way of choosing to meet the enemy in the woods to envelop them and crush them with sheer numbers. As we will see, he would combine this stratagem with the most advanced European tactics to create a hybrid force unlike any his opponents had faced.

Create Shocking Rules

As a slave, you own nothing, have no way to accumulate wealth, and can have everything, including your life and your family, taken without warning. This usually inspires overwhelmingly short-term thinking, which eradicates trust. If I am to keep my word to you rather than to pursue my short-term interests, I must believe there will be a bigger payoff from the relationship in the future than whatever I can get by betraying you now. If I believe there is no tomorrow, then there can be no trust.

This dynamic becomes problematic in an army, because trust is fundamental to running any large organization. Without trust, communication breaks. Here's why: *In any human interaction, the required amount of communication is inversely proportional to the level of trust.*

If I trust you completely, then I require no explanation or communication of your actions at all, because I know that whatever you are doing is in my best interests. On the other hand, if I don't trust you in the slightest, then no amount of talking, explaining, or reasoning will have any effect on me, because I will never believe you are telling me the truth and acting in my best interests.

As an organization grows, communication becomes its biggest challenge. If soldiers fundamentally trust the general, then communication will be vastly more efficient than if they don't.

To instill trust throughout his army, Louverture established a rule so shocking it begged the question "Why do we have that rule?" The rule forbade married officers from having concubines. As raping and pillaging were the norm for soldiers, requiring officers to respect their marital vows must have seemed absurd. One can almost hear the officers saying, "You must be kidding!" Certainly they would have demanded the rationale for this edict.

When everyone wants to know "Why?" in an organization, the answer programs the culture, because it's an answer everyone will remember. The explanation will be repeated to every new recruit and will embed itself into the cultural fabric. New officers would ask, "Tell me again why I can't have a concubine?" And be told: "Because in this army, nothing is more important than your word. If we can't trust you to keep your word to your wife, we definitely can't trust you to keep your word to us." (The matter is complicated by the fact that Louverture had illegitimate children, but no leader is perfect.)

Marriage, honesty, and loyalty were symbols of the society that Louverture aspired to lead—and he programmed them all into his culture with one simple shocking rule.

Dress for Success

When Toussaint Louverture joined the rebel army, most of its soldiers didn't wear clothes. They had joined up straight from the fields, and were accustomed to working naked. To help transform this ragtag group into an army—to give them a sense that they were an elite fighting force—Louverture and his corevolutionaries dressed in the most elaborate military uniforms attainable. It was a constant reminder of who they were and what they might achieve.

Philippe Girard writes:

> *Eager to show that they were more than a pillaging mob, the rebels took on all the trappings of a European army of the Old Regime, complete with aides-de-camp, laissez-passers, and fancy officer brevets.*

To many of Toussaint's biographers, this behavior seemed clownish and absurd. Weren't the rebels trying to destroy the Europeans and all that they stood for?

Definitely not. The rebels were trying to build an army that could set them free and a culture that could sustain their independence. So they adopted the best practices from armies that had succeeded before them. As we will see in the next chapter, something as seemingly simple as a dress code can change behavior, and therefore culture, not only in war but in business.

Incorporate Outside Leadership

A leader can transform a culture by bringing in leadership from a culture whose ways she wants to adapt. Julius Caesar did this to great effect when he built the Roman Empire. Rather than executing vanquished leaders, he often left them in place so that they could govern the region using their superior understanding of the local culture. Louverture probably absorbed this idea when he read Caesar's *Commentaries.*

Unlike Caesar, Louverture faced a situation where the oppressors and the oppressed were accustomed to pigeonholing each other by skin color. Nonetheless, he brought mulattoes into his army and incorporated deserting French royalist officers, whom he used to organize an efficient staff and train his army in the orthodox military arts. This wasn't easy—there was consternation when he showed up with white men in tow—but he insisted. When blacks told him they wouldn't obey whites or mulattoes, he would pour a glass of wine and a glass of water, then mix them together and say, "How can you tell which is which? We must all live together."

Company cultures organize around a simple goal: build

a product or service that people want. But when those companies progress beyond their initial battles they must evolve to take on new challenges. To defeat the French, Louverture needed to understand and master that culture and its military tactics, so he brought in leaders with that knowledge.

I often see companies that plan to go into new areas, but don't want to shift their culture accordingly. Many consumer companies want to penetrate the enterprise market—that is, selling to big companies—but resist having employees who walk around in fancy suits. They believe that their original culture should suffice. But their results prove otherwise.

Building a great culture means adapting it to circumstances. And that often means bringing in outside leadership from the culture you need to penetrate or master.

Make Decisions That Demonstrate Cultural Priorities

The more counterintuitive the leader's decision, the stronger the impact on the culture. Louverture set his culture by making one of the most counterintuitive decisions of the revolution.

Once the rebels won control of the island, many of Louverture's soldiers wanted revenge on the plantation owners. It would have been the course of least resistance for Louverture to order the owners shot out of hand. They would certainly have done the same to him. But he abhorred the spirit of revenge, believing it would destroy rather than elevate the culture.

He also had to fund his war against France. If his

country went bankrupt, his revolution would fail. Crops were the entire economy of Saint-Domingue: without them, it could never be an important nation. As Louverture declared, "The guarantee of the liberty of the blacks is the prosperity of agriculture." He knew that plantations had to remain large to be economically viable, and that the owners had the knowledge, education, and experience the colony needed to keep the plantations going.

So Louverture not only let the plantation owners live, he let them keep their land. But he insisted that they pay their laborers one-fourth of the profits. And he ordered them to live on their plantations, so they would be directly accountable for paying their workers and treating them well. If they disobeyed, their land was confiscated.

With these decisions, Louverture established what a thousand speeches could not have: that the revolution wasn't about revenge and that the economic well-being of the colony was its highest priority. It was all very well for him to *say* "no reprisals," but it was what he *did* that set the culture.

Walk the Talk

No culture can flourish without the enthusiastic participation of its leader. No matter how well designed, carefully programmed, and insistently enforced your cultural elements are, inconsistent or hypocritical behavior by the person in charge will blow the whole thing up.

Imagine a CEO who decides that punctuality is critical to her company's culture. She delivers eloquent speeches about how being on time is a matter of respect. She points out that employee time is the company's most valuable asset, so that when you show up late, you are effectively robbing your colleagues. But she then shows up late to all her meetings. How many employees will adhere to that value?

Louverture understood this perfectly. He asked a great deal from his soldiers, but he was more than willing to embody his own standards. He lived with the men in his army and shared their labors. If a cannon had to be moved, he pitched in, once getting a hand badly crushed in the process. He charged at his troops' head, something Europe had rarely seen from a leader since Alexander the Great, and was wounded seventeen times.

Louverture began building trust by being trustworthy himself. As C. L. R. James observed, "By his incessant activity on their behalf he gained their confidence, and among a people ignorant, starving, badgered, and nervous, Louverture's word by 1796 was law—the only person in the North whom they could be depended upon to obey."

Because the culture he wanted was a straight reflection of his own values, Louverture walked the talk better than most. His commandment against revenge was put to the test after he defeated his rival André Rigaud, a mulatto commander in the South, in the bloody War of Knives. Rigaud had not only rebelled against Louverture, but he had scoffed at the basis of his authority, proclaiming that the caste system, which put mulattoes just below whites and blacks at the bottom, was correct. Facing Rigaud's last supporters, Louverture delivered his verdict: "Forgive us our trespasses, as we forgive those who trespass against us. Return to your duty, I have already forgotten everything."

For a culture to stick, it must reflect the leader's actual values, not just those he thinks sound inspiring. Because a leader creates culture chiefly by his actions—by example.

Make Ethics Explicit

Every company likes to believe it has integrity, but if you asked its employees you'd hear a different story. The trouble with implementing integrity is that it is an abstract, long-term concept. Will integrity get you an extra deal this quarter? Unlikely. In fact, it may do the opposite. Will it make your product ship a week early? No chance. So why do we care about it?

Integrity, honesty, and decency are long-term cultural investments. Their purpose is not to make the quarter, beat a competitor, or attract a new employee. Their purpose is to create a better place to work and to make the company a better one to do business with in the long run. This value does not come for free. In the short run it may cost you deals, people, and investors, which is why most companies cannot bring themselves to actually, really, enforce it. But as we'll see, the failure to enforce good conduct often brings modern companies to their knees.

One difficulty in implementing integrity is that it's a concept without boundaries. You can't pat yourself on the back for treating your employees ethically if you're simultaneously lying to your customers, because your employees will pick up on the discrepancy and start lying to each other. The behaviors must be universal; you have to live up to them in every context.

Understanding this, Louverture painstakingly, systematically, and relentlessly moved his slave army to higher and higher levels of conduct. He was not playing a short-term game; he was determined to create an army, and then a country, that people would be proud to be a part of. Because he was determined not just to win the revolution, but to build a great country, he knew he had to take the long view.

Louverture's new state would be based on personal industry, social morality, public education, religious toleration, free trade, civic pride, and racial equality. He emphasized that attaining these goals would be each person's responsibility: "Learn, citizens, to appreciate the glory of your new political status. In acquiring the rights that the constitution affords all Frenchman, do not forget the duties it imposes on you." His instructions to his army were particularly direct: "Do not disappoint me . . . do not permit the desire for booty to turn you aside . . . it will be time enough to think of material things when we have driven the enemy from our shores. We are fighting that liberty—the most precious of earthly possessions— may not perish."

Crucially, Louverture's ethical instruction was explicit. Often CEOs will be exceptionally explicit about goals such as shipping products, but silent on matters such as obeying the law. This can be fatal. It's because integrity is often at odds with other goals that it must be clearly and specifically inserted into the culture. If a company expects its people to behave ethically without giving them detailed instructions on what that behavior looks like and how to pursue it, the company will fall far short no matter whom it hires.

This is why Louverture underlined his instructions with strict enforcement. Pamphile de Lacroix, a French general who fought against Louverture, wrote, "Never was a European army subjected to more severe discipline than that observed by Louverture's troops." The contrast with the French was stark. As C. L. R. James observed, "The soldier emigres, Dessources and some others, vicomtes, and chevaliers, broke the terms of the amnesty, destroyed cannon and ammunition dumps, killed all the animals, and set plantations on fire. Louverture's Africans, on the other hand, starving and half-naked, marched into the towns, and such was their discipline that no single act of violence or pillage was committed."

When Louverture's own army was starving during its campaign against the British, he nonetheless gave food to destitute local white women. He wrote: "My heart is torn at the fate which has befallen some unhappy whites who have been victims of this business." The women reported the assistance that they had received from this "astonishing man," and called the ugly old ex-slave their father. If you stop reading this book and go tell your friends that the slave who led the Haitian Revolution was called "Father" by the white women of the colony, they won't believe you, because it's unbelievable. But it's true. Such is the power of ethics.

By 1801, Louverture's massive investment in the culture began to pay off. With blacks and mulattoes running the country, cultivation had been restored to two-thirds of its peak level under the French. Integrity proved its worth.

WHAT HAPPENED TO LOUVERTURE?

The end of Louverture's story is dismaying. After Louverture wrote his constitution in 1801, Napoleon became furious at this display of independence and decided to overthrow him. The following year, Louverture's second in command, the fierce General Jean-Jacques Dessalines, coordinated a double cross with Napoleon's top general in Saint-Domingue. Louverture was arrested at a diplomatic meeting and sent by ship to France, where he would spend the brief remainder of his days being badly treated in a French jail. He died of a stroke and pneumonia on April 7, 1803. Meanwhile, Napoleon began restoring slavery throughout the Caribbean. It was this, in great part, that led Dessalines to turn against Napoleon. He united all rebel factions under him, defeated Napoleon's army, and declared independence in January 1804. He changed the country's name to Haiti, and later that year had himself proclaimed emperor.

Dessalines completed the revolution that Louverture had spearheaded for so long, but he promptly made two decisions that Louverture would have abhorred: he ordered that most of the French whites in Haiti be put to death and he nationalized all private land, abruptly reversing much of the cultural and economic headway that Louverture had made. Though the French would eventually give Haiti diplomatic recognition in 1825, they would also exact cruel reparations for Dessalines's shortsighted decisions, forcing Haiti to pay the modern equivalent of $21 billion for France's loss of its slaves and plantations. These events continue to haunt the country, which remains the poorest in the Western world.

Sad story, but how could it happen? How could Louverture, genius of culture and human nature that he was, not perceive the brewing treachery? In a sense, he was like the Greek hero Oedipus, who solved the riddle of the Sphinx but who couldn't clearly see those closest to him. Louverture's optimistic view of human potential blinded him to certain home truths.

Because Louverture believed in the French Revolution and the freedoms it claimed to embody, he saw Napoleon as an enlightened product of the revolution rather than as the racist he was. In one outburst, Napoleon said: "I will not rest until I have torn the epaulettes off every nigger in the colonies."

Because of Louverture's loyalty to France, he didn't declare independence when the French army invaded, which would have united the whole island behind him. He vacillated.

And because Louverture trusted—all too much—that his army would trust him to act for the best, he didn't grasp that his soldiers were restless about everything from his position on agriculture to his constant efforts to attain a diplomatic solution with France, to his rule against revenge. Louverture did not grasp the emotional power of retribution, whereas Dessalines did.

C. L. R. James put it well: "If Dessalines could see so clearly and simply, it was because the ties that bound this uneducated soldier to French civilization were of the slenderest. He saw what was right under his nose so well because he saw no further. Louverture's failure was the failure of enlightenment, not darkness."

Yet though Louverture's culture proved tragically difficult for his flawed subordinate to live up to, it had an enduring power. After Napoleon captured Louverture, he attempted to reinstitute slavery on the island—but was beaten by the army Louverture left behind. Though he was already dead, Louverture defeated his third European superpower. Napoleon suffered more losses in Saint-Domingue than he would at Waterloo, and these reverses forced him to sell Louisiana and parts of fourteen additional states to the United States for $15 million. The French emperor later confessed that he should have ruled the island through Louverture.

HISTORICAL IMPACT

The slave revolution of Saint-Domingue got into the area's bloodstream and spread from island to island in the Caribbean. Later rebellions in Brazil, Colombia, Venezuela,

Curacao, Guadeloupe, Puerto Rico, Cuba, and Louisiana were attributable, at least in part, to Haitian agents and their followers. These rebellions influenced the eventual withdrawal of the French, British, and Spanish empires from the region.

In the United States, Louverture inspired the abolitionist John Brown to launch the raid on the armory at Harpers Ferry, which Brown hoped would prompt the local slaves to rebel. The attack failed and Brown was hanged, but the Harpers Ferry raid escalated tensions that, a year later, led to the South's secession and the Civil War.

While one of the greatest culture geniuses in history was unable to permanently establish the way of life he hoped for in his home country, he helped shift the Western world from a culture of slavery to one of freedom.

Toussaint Louverture made missteps that locked him up for life, yet he helped liberate us all.

2 TOUSSAINT LOUVERTURE APPLIED

I'm a murderer, n*gg*, but I don't promote violence.
—*Gucci Mane*

The techniques Louverture used with rare ingenuity and skill work brilliantly at modern companies.

KEEP WHAT WORKS

When Steve Jobs returned to run Apple in 1997, the company was in bad shape. Really bad shape. Its market share had fallen from 13 percent when Jobs was fired in 1985 to 3.3 percent, and it was only a quarter's worth of cash from insolvency. When rival computer maker Michael Dell was asked what should be done with Apple, he said, "I'd shut it down and give the money back to the shareholders."

Even within Apple, almost everyone believed the conventional wisdom that the company's death spiral resulted from what was known as personal computer economics. The theory of PC economics held that because the industry had commoditized PC hardware—there were IBM knockoffs everywhere—the way to make money was not to be a vertically integrated provider that gave the user the machine and its operating system, but to focus on the horizontal option: selling an operating system to run on someone else's hardware.

Nearly every analyst was pushing Apple to make its Mac OS operating system the company's product. In 1997, *Wired* proclaimed: "Admit it. You're out of the hardware game." Even Apple's cofounder, Steve Wozniak, subscribed to this view: "We had the most beautiful operating system," he said, "but to get it you had to buy our hardware at twice the price. That was a mistake."

Steve Jobs disregarded that advice. In fact, one of his first acts as CEO was to stop licensing Mac OS to other hardware providers.

The industry's other article of faith was that companies needed to maximize market share by having a presence in every link of the computer chain, from servers to printers to PCs to laptops. Likewise, they needed to make PCs in all shapes and sizes for every possible user. But Jobs immediately killed the majority of Apple's products, including most of its PC models, as well as all of its servers and printers and its Newton handheld computer.

Why? Jobs saw the situation entirely differently. At an early all-hands meeting he asked, "Okay, tell me what's wrong with this place?" He answered his own question: "It's the products!" He went on to inquire, "So what's wrong with the products?" and to answer himself again: "The products suck!"

For Jobs, the issue was not the economic structure of the PC industry. Apple just needed to build better products. He would need to transform its culture to make that happen, but it would only happen if he built upon Apple's strengths, not Microsoft's.

Integrating hardware and software had always been Apple's core strength. At its peak, the company had focused not on industry benchmarks like processor speeds and storage capacity, but on building products such as the MacIntosh that encouraged people's creativity. Apple did integration better than anyone else. Part of the magic was its ability to control the entire product, from the user interface to the precise color of the hardware. Jobs went out of his way to keep the employees who understood this, user-experience perfectionists like him. Jobs said about one such employee, the great designer Jony Ive, "He understands what we do at our core better than anyone."

The company's famous Think Different advertising campaign, which launched in 1997, featured creative geniuses such as Gandhi, John Lennon, and Albert Einstein. Jobs explained: "We at Apple had forgotten who we were. One way to remember who you are is to remember who your heroes are." For Apple to become great again, it had to build on the aspect of its culture that had distinguished it in the past.

Jobs narrowed the product line to ensure that the company focused on delivering great experiences to individual humans rather than an impersonal set of specs, feeds, and speeds aimed at no one in particular. Over time, he would expand to include iPods, iPads, and iPhones, but he never went "horizontal"—he kept the software and hardware integrated. To further control the customer experience, Jobs even opened Apple Stores, which would become one of the best-performing retail businesses in the world.

When Steve Jobs came back to Apple, it was ninety days from broke. As of this writing, it is the most valuable company in the world.

When Apple was an industry joke, it must have been tempting to purge the old culture entirely. Jobs's predecessor, Gil Amelio, tried to do just that. But like Louverture, the former slave who preserved the best parts of slave culture within his army, Jobs, the former founder, knew that Apple's original strengths should be the foundation of its new mission.

CREATE SHOCKING RULES

Here are the rules for writing a rule so powerful it sets the culture for many years:

- *It must be memorable.* If people forget the rule, they forget the culture.

- *It must raise the question "Why?"* Your rule should be so bizarre and shocking that everybody who hears it is compelled to ask, "Are you serious?"
- *Its cultural impact must be straightforward.* The answer to the "Why?" must clearly explain the cultural concept.
- *People must encounter the rule almost daily.* If your incredibly memorable rule applies only to situations people face once a year, it's irrelevant.

When Tom Coughlin coached the New York Giants, from 2004 to 2015, the media went crazy over a shocking rule he set: *If you are on time, you are late.* He started every meeting five minutes early and fined players one thousand dollars if they were late. I mean on time. Wait, what?

At first, the "Coughlin Time" rule went over poorly. Several players filed grievances with the NFL and the *New York Times* wrote a scathing critique:

> In the player-relations department, the reign of Giants Coach Tom Coughlin started poorly and is already showing signs of unraveling one game into the season.
>
> On the heels of Sunday's 31–17 loss to the Eagles, the N.F.L. Players Association confirmed that three Giants had filed a grievance against Coughlin for fining them for not being early enough for a meeting.
>
> A few weeks ago, linebackers Carlos Emmons and Barrett Green and cornerback Terry Cousin, all free-agent

*acquisitions in the off-season, were fined $1,000 each af-
ter showing up several minutes early for a meeting, only
to be told they needed to arrive earlier.*

Coughlin's response to the reporter didn't make him
seem more sympathetic, but it did solidify his rule:
"Players ought to be there on time, period," he said. "If
they're on time, they're on time. Meetings start five minutes early."

Was the rule memorable? Check. Did it beg the question "Why?" He had players asking everyone from the
league to the *New York Times* "Why?" so, check. Did they
encounter it daily? Yep, they ran into it every time they
had to be somewhere. But what was he trying to achieve?

Eleven years and two Super Bowl wins later, backup
quarterback Ryan Nassib explained the cultural intention to the *Wall Street Journal*:

*Coughlin Time is more of a mindset, kind of a way for
players to discipline themselves, making sure they're
on time, making sure they're attentive and making sure
they're ready to work when it's time to start meetings.
It's actually kind of nice because once you get out in
the real world, you're five minutes early to everything.*

In business, creating partnerships that work is a difficult
art. Success stories such as the partnership of Microsoft
and Intel or of Siebel Systems and Accenture become
legendary, but for every success there are a hundred fail-
ures. It's difficult enough to align interests in your own

organization, where everyone works for you, but doing it between companies is close to impossible.

In the 1980s, the business literature promoted the concept of win-win partnerships. Unfortunately, the idea was pretty abstract. How do you know if a deal is win-win? Can you actually determine when it's fifty-fifty? The idea also failed to address the cultural adjustment required: if everything in a business culture is about winning, what behavior changes are necessary to achieve a win-win mindset? Finally, its meaning was easy to twist. Devious negotiators routinely said, "We want this to be a win-win."

In 1998, Diane Greene cofounded a virtualized operating system company, VMware, whose success depended on her partnership strategy. But she was entering a field that had witnessed the biggest win-lose partnership ever—Microsoft winning total dominance by "partnering" with IBM on the desktop operating system. VMware's potential partners would be extremely skeptical of any independent-operating-system company proposing a similar "win-win."

So Greene came up with a shocking rule: *Partnerships should be 49/51, with VMware getting the 49.* Did she just tell her team to lose? That definitely begs the question "Why?"

Greene said, "I had to give our business development people permission to be good to the partners, because one-sided partnerships would not work." Her rule was actually met not with resistance but with relief. Her people wanted to create mutually beneficial partnerships, and

Greene's rule gave them permission. It was of course no easier to measure an exact 49/51 split than a 50/50 "win-win," but Greene's employees understood her underlying point: "If you're negotiating something on the margin, it's okay to give it to our partner." VMware went on to create a stunning set of partnerships with Intel, Dell, HP, and IBM that propelled the company to a market capitalization of more than $60 billion.

One of the most distinctive large-company cultures is Amazon's. It promulgates its fourteen cultural values in a number of ways, but perhaps most effectively through a few shocking rules. One value, frugality, is defined as *Accomplish more with less. Constraints breed resourcefulness, self-sufficiency, and invention. There are no extra points for growing head count, budget size, or fixed expenses.*

That's a nice definition, but how do you drive home that you mean it? Here's how: desks at Amazon were built by buying cheap doors from Home Depot and nailing legs to them. These door desks weren't great ergonomically, but when a shocked new employee asked why she had to work at a makeshift desk, the answer pinged back with illuminating consistency: "We look for every opportunity to save money so we can deliver the best products for the lowest cost." (Amazon no longer gives everyone a door desk, as the culture has now been set—and as there are cheaper alternatives.)

Some of Amazon's values are fairly abstract. *Dive deep*, for instance, encourages leaders to operate at all levels, stay connected to the details, audit frequently, and investigate more thoroughly when metrics and anecdotal evidence disagree.

Great idea—but how do you drive this kind of thoughtfulness into the culture? The shocking rule that helps is *No PowerPoint presentations in meetings.* In an industry where presentations rule the day, this rule definitely counts as shocking. To convene a meeting at Amazon, you must prepare a short written document explaining the issues to be discussed and your position on them. When the meeting begins everyone silently reads the document. Then the discussion starts, with everyone up to speed on a shared set of background information.

Amazon executive Ariel Kelman explains that the rule makes meetings much more efficient:

> *If you have to talk about something complicated, you want to load the data into people's brains as quickly as possible so you can have an intelligent, facts-based conversation about the business decision you're trying to make.*
>
> *So, say you're meeting to figure out pricing for a new product, you've got to talk about the cost structure, how much is fixed, how much is variable, and then there might be three different pricing models, each with pros and cons. That's a lot of information. Now, you can sit and listen to someone pitch all of this information, but most people don't have the patience to pay attention long enough to be effective in absorbing all of this data and it typically takes too much time. There's been a lot of research done on this that shows that most people's*

brains can absorb new information several times faster and more effectively by reading information versus listening to it. Also, asking people to present their plans in written format forces them to express their ideas with a deeper level of detail.

A culture is a set of actions. By requiring thoughtful action before every meeting, Amazon moves its culture in the right direction every day.

In the early days of Facebook, Mark Zuckerberg was keenly aware that the more people he got on his network, the better his product would be. As MySpace had far more users, Facebook had to outgrow them by building better software—software that had better features, was more user-friendly, and that excelled at identifying potential new Facebook users. Zuckerberg knew that he didn't have much time: if MySpace got big enough, it might transform from an entertaining application into an invincible utility.

Speed was the number one virtue he needed, so he created a shocking rule: *Move fast and break things.* Imagine you are an engineer hearing that for the first time: Break things? I thought the point was to make things. Why is Mark telling us to break things? Well, he's telling you so that when you come up with an innovative product and you are not sure whether it's worth potentially destabilizing the code base to push the product along, you already have your answer. Moving fast is the virtue; breaking things is the acceptable by-product. Zuckerberg later observed that the reason the rule was so powerful was that it stated not only what Facebook wanted, but what it would give up to get it.

After Facebook caught and passed MySpace, it had new missions to pursue, such as turning the social network into a platform. At that point, the *move fast* virtue became more liability than asset. When outside developers tried to build applications on Facebook, the underlying platform kept breaking, which jeopardized the businesses of Facebook's partners. So in 2014 Zuckerberg replaced his by-now-famous rule with the boring but stage-appropriate motto *Move fast with stable infrastructure.* Cultures must evolve with the mission.

When Marissa Mayer became CEO of Yahoo! in 2012, its reputation was of a company whose workforce didn't give its all. She knew that to compete with her old company, Google, she would need a better effort from the team. She began by trying to lead by example, working relentlessly long hours. Yet she kept arriving at work to see an empty parking lot.

So in 2013, Mayer created a rule so shocking that it created massive backlash not only inside but even *outside* the company: during work hours, you must be at work. *Nobody is allowed to work from home.* But this was the technology industry—the industry that had invented the tools that enabled people to work from home! As the world exploded in anger, Mayer calmly explained her position. She had examined the virtual private networking logs of employees who were working from home; they had to use the VPN to securely access their work files. The logs showed that most people "working from home" had in fact not been working at all.

She shocked people because she had to make a dramatic cultural change. It's worth nothing that while Mayer succeeded in building assiduousness back into Yahoo!'s culture, she never quite turned the company around. That's the nature of culture—it helps you do what you are doing better, but it can't fix your strategy or thwart a dominant competitor.

DRESS FOR SUCCESS

When Mary Barra took over as the CEO of General Motors in 2014, she wanted to dismantle the company's powerful bureaucracy. It stifled employees and disempowered managers: rather than communicating with employees and giving them guidance, the managers relied on the extensive system of rules to do the job for them. The ten-page dress code was the worst example. To shock the system and change the culture, Barra reduced ten pages to two words: dress appropriately.

She told the story at the Wharton People Analytics Conference:

The HR department started arguing with me, saying, it can be "Dress appropriately" on the surface, but in the employee manual it needs to be a lot more detailed.

They put in specifics like, "Don't wear T-shirts that say inappropriate things, or statements that could be misinterpreted."

Barra was perplexed.

"What does inappropriate, in the context of a T-shirt, even mean?" she asked the audience, half-jokingly.

So I finally had to say, "No, it's two words, that's what I want." What followed was really a window into the company for me.

Barra promptly received an email from a senior-level director:

He said, "You need to put out a better dress policy, this is not enough." So I called him—and of course that shook him a little bit. And I asked him to help me understand why the policy was inept.

The director explained that some people on his team occasionally had to deal with government officials on short notice, and they needed to be dressed appropriately for that.

"Okay, why don't you talk to your team," I replied. He was an established leader at GM, responsible for a pretty important part of the company, with a multimillion-dollar budget. He called me back a few minutes later, saying, "I talked to the team, we brainstormed, and we agreed that the four people who occasionally need to

*meet with government officials will keep a pair of dress
pants in their locker." Problem solved.*

The change sent a lasting visual message to GM's entire
management team. Every time a manager saw an employee,
it would trigger the thought, Is he dressed appropriately?
And, if not, What's the best way for me to manage that? Do
I have a good enough relationship with him to commu-
nicate effectively on this sensitive issue? The new code
empowered—and required—managers to manage.

When Michael Ovitz ran Creative Artists Agency, Hollywood's leading talent agency, he, too, had no explicit
dress code. But he absolutely had an implicit one. "In
the mid-seventies, we lived in a world coming off sixties
culture, where everyone wore jeans and T-shirts," Ovitz
recalled. "That's what I needed to counter-program." The
dress code he landed on came from the culture of authority he sought: "If you walk into the room wearing an
elegant dark suit, you pick up unbelievable positioning
power. If you want respect, carry yourself in a way that
commands it."

Ovitz wore elegant dark suits every day, leading by
example. He never explicitly asked anyone to follow
his lead. That didn't mean there weren't consequences
if you didn't. "There was a downpour in LA, and some
people came in in rain boots and jeans. I went up to one
agent and said, 'Nice outfit. Are you working on set today?' And that rattled through our business." Ovitz was
giving him the hip-hop ultimatum: Are you a hustler or

a customer? Are you a world-class agent or a wannabe actor? This steely but largely unspoken approach soon shifted CAA to nearly complete dress code compliance. "The only exception was our music department, because musicians don't like guys in suits."

The results of the code on the culture were profound:

It became part of our ethos: we were classy, elegant, conservative businesspeople. It spoke to everything we wanted to be without our having to say it out loud. Through our culture we built our business to a place where people respected it due to the culture itself.

How you dress, the most visible thing you do, can be the most important invisible force driving your organization's behavior. Ovitz sums it up: "Cultures are shaped more by the invisible than the visible. They are willed."

INCORPORATE OUTSIDE LEADERSHIP—HEY, MOTHERFUCKER!

When I was CEO of LoudCloud, I had to shift the company from a high-flying cloud services company into a grind-'em-out enterprise software company so we could survive. After the dot-com and telecom crashes of the early 2000s, the market for cloud services had gone from nearly infinite to nearly zero overnight. After we squeaked through the transition as a new company called Opsware, we found ourselves getting killed in the software market by a competitor named BladeLogic. I knew that to compete with them we needed a major cultural change.

At LoudCloud, we began with unlimited demand and built a culture oriented around fulfilling it. So we were focused on empowerment, removing bottlenecks to growth, and being a great place to work. To succeed as an enterprise software company, selling our platform to big businesses, we would have to become a culture distinguished by urgency, competitiveness, and precision. I needed to bring in a leader with those attributes.

The person I hired as our head of sales, Mark Cranney, was not a cultural fit with the rest of us. In fact, he was a complete cultural misfit. Our employees were mostly irreligious Democrats from the west coast who dressed casually and who were cordial and easygoing. We assumed that everyone had the best intentions. Cranney was a Mormon Republican from Boston who wore a suit and tie, was deeply suspicious of everyone, and was one of the most competitive people on earth. But over the next four years he not only saved the company, but got us to an outcome nobody would have believed.

I knew why I hired Mark: when I interviewed him, I could tell he had the urgency, the know-how, and the discipline we needed. But I did not understand why he took the job. He knew we were losing and, given our granola-eating demographics, that we were probably losers. So what made him take the risk? I recently asked him, and his reason surprised me:

I had risen as far as I could at an east-coast-based company called PTC; they had nepotistic politics at the top level. I must have looked at forty sales jobs in Boston and there was nothing good.

The Opsware recruiter called several times and I finally called him back and said, "I'm not going to California. In California the real estate sucks, the culture sucks, and they don't appreciate the sales side. Plus, isn't that the company the BladeLogic guys call Oopsware? What do you think, I'm fuckin' stupid?"

He keeps calling and finally, I say "Fine, I'll go meet Marc and Ben, but that's it." [Marc Andreessen was the company's cofounder.] Then I look at my BlackBerry when I land in San Francisco and I see there's a whole fucking crew I have to interview with.

So I go over and you come out of your cubicle and I'm like, Fucking cube company. The cubes confirmed my initial suspicions: soft, beach boys, consensus, everyone gets a say. That's fine for engineering, but sales and marketing have to go to battle every day, so people in those groups need to fall in line. Then I'm looking at the conference room names—Salt-N-Pepa, Notorious B.I.G.—and I'm like, What the fuck are these? When I realize they're the names of rappers I think, Jeez, this is not going to go well.

We sat down and I said, "Ben, before we get started I need to know what your process is and what your decision criteria are. You've got all these people interviewing me and if they all get a vote then it kind of explains why you're in the situation you're in." You got up out of your seat and said, "Hey, motherfucker! I'm the CEO. I make the decisions." When you said "Hey, motherfucker!" I said to myself, Wait a minute. Maybe I can do this.

I was stunned. That was it? Hey, motherfucker? It was weird, but profound. By being willing, in that moment, to see Mark for who he was and to go meet him in his culture, I made him just comfortable enough that he took a chance on us.

We got him in the nick of time. Not only did we lack an enterprise sales culture, but we lacked everything that underpinned it: a sales philosophy, methodology, and attitude. We needed an approach to winning deals, a method that would reliably make us stand out, and an attitude that we would refuse to lose. Cranney had all of that. It started with his philosophy. He believed that you were either selling or being sold: if you weren't selling a customer on your product then the customer was selling you on why she wasn't going to buy it.

He instilled in our eight-person sales team the crucial four C's. To sell, you had have 1) the *competence*—expert knowledge of the product you were selling and the process to demonstrate it (qualifying the buyer by validating their need and budget; helping define what their buying criteria are while setting traps for the competition; getting sign-off from the technical and the economic buyer at the customer, and so forth) so that you could have 2) the *confidence* to state your point of view, which would give you 3) the *courage* to have 4) the *conviction* not to be sold by the customer on why she wasn't going to buy your product. Cranney was obsessed with training every salesperson, testing them, and holding them accountable on the four C's.

For him, selling was a team sport. That sounds like he made it fun and collegial, but no. He was fond of saying that most reps had a *Wizard of Oz* problem: they lacked either the courage, the brain, or the heart to be success-ful by themselves. That's where the process and the team came into play. Every person on each sales team had a specific role to play—making the technical sale, navigating the organization, serving as the closer—and if he did not play his role to perfection, the sale was in jeopardy. Quite rapidly, Cranney's system began to work. In his first nine months, our sales team expanded to thirty people and our win rate went from the low 40s to the mid-80s.

As he saw sales as analogous to football, he kept a close eye on the clock and the scoreboard. His urgency and his total intolerance for anyone who was hurting our ef-fort caused more than a few clashes with his team. Early on, he went to Memphis to observe one of our technical proofs of concept (POCs) at FedEx, where we installed our software in a company's environment to prove that we could manage their servers as advertised. POCs were complex and stressful, because of the extreme variance in network equipment types, servers, and software. Chip Starkey, one of our best field engineers, was running this one, and Cranney asked him where Mike the sales rep was. Chip said, "He never attends these." Cranney took out his phone:

MARK: Mike, did you get a good workout in today?
MIKE: Yes, I ran five miles.
MARK: Good news! You're going to have a lot more time to work out, because you're fired.

Two months into Cranney's tenure, I received a call from Sy Lorne, a board member who chaired our governance committee and had helped to design our whistleblower policy. Sy was a brilliant lawyer who had been the general counsel of the Securities and Exchange Commission:

SY: Ben, I received a somewhat disturbing letter.
BEN: [highly alarmed] What did it say?
SY: "Dear Mr. Lorne, I am writing to you in your capacity as the point of escalation on Opsware's whistleblower procedures. I recently interviewed at Opsware and must report my experience. Everyone at Opsware was extremely professional, well-mannered, and courteous throughout the process. Everybody except Mark Cranney. In my entire career, I have never experienced such a lack of professionalism or decency. I request that you fire Mr. Cranney immediately. Sincerely, [name removed to protect the innocent]."
BEN: Did he say what happened?
SY: No, that's the whole letter.
BEN: What do you think I should do?

SY: Well, you have to investigate it. Once you do, let's talk again.

I called my head of human resources, Shannon Schiltz. Unlike many HR professionals, Shannon did not engage in politics. She moved in silence with precise intent, like a ninja. I said: "Shannon, I need you to investigate this incident with Mark, but try not to trigger his paranoia. Let's interview him last and only if necessary." She said, "I got it."

After three days, Shannon reported back. She had spoken to everyone involved in the incident, including the alleged victim, but amazingly, nobody else in the company, including Cranney, had learned about her investigation. I said, "Give me all the bad news. Don't hold anything back." She said, "Well, the good news is that the stories are one hundred percent consistent, so I really don't even need to talk to Cranney to understand what happened." I was shocked. In all the investigations that I've ever seen, the only certainty is that the stories will conflict. I asked her what happened. She said:

The candidate had experience as an inside sales rep, but not much yet as an outside rep. [In enterprise software, an outside sales rep is a more senior position.] He interviewed with various people, then with Cranney. Five minutes into the interview, Mark said: "Okay, we're done." Then, before the candidate was out of the cube, Mark crumpled up his resume and threw it in the trash. Next, before he was out of earshot, Mark

stuck his head out of his cube and yelled to the hiring
manager, "How in the fuck did that sorry motherfucker
make it all the way to me?"

I hesitated. I wanted an intensely competitive culture,
but had I gone too far? Maybe, but this was wartime—we
had to become ferocious fast. I called Sy to get his take.
He heard the whole story and said, "That's crazy." I asked,
"Do I need to fire him?" He said, "No, no. But you might
want to talk to him and have him work in a soundproof
booth."

We had an egalitarian culture borrowed from the early
days of Intel: all employees, including me, sat in cubes.
Based on Sy's advice, I sat Mark down and walked him
through the incident, explaining that he was creating liability for the company and himself. He understood the
issue, but he was who he was. So I broke our cultural
rule and put Mark in a walled office; that way if he did
slip up—and he certainly would—it wouldn't be public.
Equality was less important than the cultural virtues we
needed to survive.

We grew our valuation from around $50 million when
we hired Mark to $1.65 billion four years later, when we
sold to Hewlett-Packard. That price was roughly double
what BladeLogic sold for. Adding Cranney's cultural elements made a huge difference.

We don't have records of all the ways the soldiers of
Louverture's slave army reacted when he brought in white
French and Spanish officers, but we know that there was
tremendous tension. If you bring in outside leadership, it

will make everyone highly uncomfortable. That's what cultural change feels like.

MAKE DECISIONS THAT DEMONSTRATE PRIORITIES

In 1985, Reed Hastings was a twenty-four-year-old high school math teacher who really wanted to work with computers. He took a job serving coffee at a company called Symbolics Inc. just to get a foot in the door.

Symbolics, which registered the first dot-com ever, Symbolics.com, made the programming language LISP. LISP was elegant and easier to use than its counterparts like C. It achieved this elegance in part by shielding the programmer from managing the computer's memory, which at the time was an unbearably slow task. Symbolics had to make specialized hardware just to run the language. But when Hastings wasn't busy dispensing coffee, he learned to program the Symbolics machines.

Later, when he got his master's degree in computer science at Stanford University, he had to revert to using C. Frustrated, he began to look into managing memory more cleverly so he could improve LISP and get back to using it all the time—and he discovered techniques that made C radically easier to debug.

In those days, the most vexing software bug was a "memory leak." Memory leaks occurred when a programmer allocated the computer's memory for some temporary use, but forgot to give it back to the machine later. Because these leaks only occurred when users took a random, unpredictable path, they were exceptionally difficult to re-create and to fix—and, in the meantime, the machine was useless.

Hastings figured out a way to detect memory leaks in the lab before a program shipped, and in 1991 he started a company called Pure Software to capitalize on his discovery. Its product, Purify, radically improved the way people developed software and was a hit.

Yet he had never paid any attention to management or culture and as the head count grew, morale plunged—so much so that he asked his board to replace him as CEO (it refused). Every time Pure had a cultural problem, it aggressively put a process in place to fix it, just as though the company were maximizing semiconductor yield. The side effect of creating a massive set of rules that governed behavior—of optimizing for removing all errors rather than for encouraging exploration and free thinking—was to stifle creativity. Hastings vowed not to make that mistake again.

Pure went public in 1995 and was sold to Rational Software in 1997 for about $500 million, which gave Hastings the capital to start a company called Netflix.

Why would this computer genius start a media company?

At Stanford, Hastings had taken a course that required him to calculate the bandwidth for a computer network. This particular network was a station wagon carrying a trunk full of backup disks traveling across the country. This out-of-the-box example forced him to think about networks in a different way.

In 1997, when a friend showed him one of the first DVDs, Hastings thought, Oh, my God! This is the station wagon! That insight prompted him to build what he thought of as a high-latency, high-bandwidth computer network that delivered 5GB data payloads for a thirty-two cent postage stamp. In other words, he started a company to deliver movies over the postal network.

He knew that the network would eventually move to a low-latency, high-bandwidth equivalent, streaming its content over the Internet; that's why he called the company Netflix rather than DVD By Mail. But in 1997, the Internet was far from ready for that. Its video images were tiny, jumpy, and pretty much totally unwatchable.

So Netflix became a DVD-by-mail company that competed with Blockbuster and Walmart. In 2005, Hastings and his team saw YouTube for the first time. The quality wasn't ideal, but you could pick from a menu of videos, click on one, and watch it immediately.

Two years later, Netflix launched its streaming service. Hastings later observed that the challenge wasn't getting into a new business—almost every company could and would do that; it's B School 101. The challenge was getting into a new business with the intention of making it *the* business. Almost no companies did that. Netflix's entire high-customer-satisfaction, very-profitable culture was built around delivering DVDs.

In 2010, Hastings felt that he had just enough streaming content to run an experiment in Canada, which had no DVD-by-mail service. The company signed up as many Canadian streaming subscribers in three days as it had expected to get in three months. The age of streaming was clearly at hand—but how could Hastings make the jump to becoming a global business built around streaming? Obviously he'd have to bundle streaming with DVD to begin with, but what next? Every time he raised this vital topic with his team, trying to hyperleap the company into the future, the conversation reverted to optimizing the DVD service.

Hastings made a hard decision to demonstrate his priorities. He kicked all the executives who ran the DVD business out of his weekly management meeting. "That was one of the most painful moments in building the company," he said later. "Because we loved them, we'd grown up with them, and they're running everything that's important. But they weren't adding value in terms of the streaming discussion." Hastings had long kept looking over his shoulder for a pure-streaming company that would run right by Netflix. He knew that that competitor wouldn't have any DVD execs in its meetings. So why should Netflix, if it was going to be that company?

You'd be hard-pressed to find a management book that recommends rewarding the loyal team generating all your revenue by booting them out of the company's key meeting. But Hastings understood that moving the culture in the right direction trumped all other priorities. He had to shift the culture from one that prioritized content and logistics to one that prioritized content and technology. That change would affect everything from work hours to compensation strategy. But if he didn't make it, Netflix would today be Blockbuster—which went bankrupt in 2010.

Louverture knew that telling people that agriculture was a priority wouldn't make it so. He had to do something dramatic to demonstrate that it was the *highest* priority—something everyone would remember. He forgave the slave owners and let them keep their land. Nothing could be clearer. Likewise, Hastings couldn't just say that streaming was a priority; he had to demonstrate it.

The results for Netflix have been spectacular. As late as 2010, it was ridiculed by the media giants. "It's a little bit like, is the Albanian army going to take over the world?" said Jeffrey Bewkes, the CEO of Time Warner. "I don't think so." Today, with a market cap of more than $150 billion, Netflix is worth almost double what AT&T recently paid for Time Warner.

WALK THE TALK

The 2016 U.S. presidential election featured a blizzard of withering exposés. The press revealed Donald Trump's multiple past bankruptcies, shabby treatment of employees, and the lewd and misogynistic comments he'd made while preparing to tape a segment for *Access Hollywood*. But the most consequential attack addressed how Hillary Clinton had handled top-secret emails. This charge had real traction, climaxing in a chant of "lock her up" at the Republican National Convention—in a call to convict Clinton of espionage and other crimes. Law enforcement never came close to considering her conduct criminal, but the political damage was significant.

As secretary of state, Clinton used a personal email server instead of the government system to send and receive emails. Her enemies suggested that she must therefore have been funneling secret documents to America's enemies. Her friends, and Clinton herself, said it was simply a matter of convenience; after all, no secretary of state before John Kerry had employed a state.gov email address. Colin Powell used an AOL account.

Anyone who's had to deal with multiple email accounts on multiple mobile devices could understand Clinton's rationale. FBI investigators accepted Mrs. Clinton's explanation, taking her point that none of the emails she sent or received on her public server was marked as classified. However, that wasn't the end of her email problems.

As the election grew closer, the Russians stole a treasure trove of the Democratic Party's emails by hacking the account of John Podesta, the chairman of Clinton's campaign. This hack, and the slow drip of consequences from it, may have swung the election to Donald Trump. How did the Russians pull off this coup? Was this an audacious cyber-crime?

CyberScoop, a cyber-security news organization, explained what happened:

> Podesta wasn't hacked because he used a bad password. His email was breached because hackers sent a spear phishing email pretending to be Google asking for his credentials because, according to the fake

email, he had already been hacked. It's a common tactic of hackers to create emotional urgency during an attack. Ironic as it is, pretending you've already been hacked is a common tactic because it can push people to quickly click malicious links without thinking through or checking the consequences.

In other words, Podesta was hacked in the simplest and most common way—via an email that told him to click on a link to protect himself. Anybody who's read the most cursory article about Internet security knows that the first rule is, *Don't click on an unknown link and enter your password.* A legitimate business will *never* ask you to do it. So how could this happen?

The official story is that Podesta forwarded the suspicious email to the campaign's IT person asking whether it was legitimate and that person told campaign aide Charles Delavan that it was a phishing attack. Then Delavan mistyped in his note to Podesta, saying it was "a legitimate email" and that Podesta should "change his password immediately." Should we believe this explanation? This would be the equivalent of a suicide hotline chat where the hotline rep mistypes that the person at risk should swallow the bottle of pills and wash them down with a fifth of tequila.

So the entire episode got blamed on a low-level aide who wouldn't be attacked by the press and the Democratic Party. Hmm. In the end, though, it's irrelevant whether that story was a cover-up. What matters is that the Russians hacked Podesta's email, which revealed a number of mildly embarrassing and cumulatively damaging episodes that included campaign staffers having been fed some debate questions in advance, having gotten improper information from the Department of Justice about Clinton's email case, and joking about the hearings into the Benghazi attack of 2012.

In her book about the campaign, *What Happened*, Clinton recognized that questions about her personal handling of emails—as pointed out in former FBI director James Comey's inflammatory letter to Congress about them just ten days before the election—were compounded by the Podesta hack: "Together, the effects of Comey's letter and the Russian attack formed a devastating combination."

How could the campaign have been so negligent?

Whether you were a Clinton supporter (as I was) or a detractor, most reasonable people would agree that she was an experienced and competent manager. Her campaign's explicit instructions to all staff were to take security very seriously. In late March 2015, FBI agents visited her campaign managers to warn that foreign governments would try phishing them. Everyone was required to use two-factor authentication on their email accounts and every member of the campaign was trained on phishing attacks. If Podesta had followed either of those protocols he would have fended off the attack. Together, the protocols formed the standard belt-and-suspenders-level protection.

But there was a flaw in the plan. Two-factor authentication was required on everyone's *work* email. The phishing attack was sent to Podesta's *personal* email. Now, what past behavior could possibly have given Podesta the idea that he could send and receive tons of highly confidential campaign emails from his personal email account? Oh, snap.

Not once did Hillary Clinton tell John Podesta, "Don't take email security seriously." Not once would she *ever* have told him that. But Clinton's actions overrode her intentions. It did not matter that the campaign had taken all the steps necessary to prevent the attack, because John Podesta imitated what Hillary Clinton did, not what she said. The talk said, "Secure your email"; the walk said, "Personal convenience is more important." The walk almost always wins. That's how culture works.

Before condemning Clinton for this catastrophic error, keep in mind that every leader will make decisions she later regrets. Nobody has ever been close to perfect. Furthermore, it is a common and understandable mistake to think of cyber security as an isolated function that, like processing payroll, has no bearing on the larger culture. In fact, the most important aspects of an organization's performance—quality, design, security, fiscal discipline, customer care—are all culturally driven.

When you inevitably take an action that's inconsistent with your culture, the best fix is to admit it, then move to overcorrect the error. The admission and the self-correction have to be public enough and vehement enough to erase the earlier decision and become the new lesson.

Clinton seems never to have contemplated this kind of admission and course correction; an ironclad rule of U.S. politics is "Never admit you were wrong." (This rule is one reason why it's hard to wholeheartedly admire most politicians.) In her book, she accepts some blame for her carelessness, but shrugs off most of the responsibility: "one boneheaded mistake turned into a campaign-defining and -destroying scandal, thanks to a toxic mix of partisan opportunism, interagency turf battles, a rash FBI director, my own inability to explain the whole mess in a way people could understand, and media coverage that by its very volume told the voters this was by far the most important issue of the campaign."

She then writes of the leaked Podesta emails, "None of this had anything at all to do with my use of personal email at the State Department—nothing at all—but for many voters, it would all blend together." The two email screwups were indeed unrelated in the sense that Clinton means—but totally related in the sense that I mean. While it's likely that the Democratic Party's emails would have been hacked even if Clinton hadn't been dismissive of email security, the point is that when you are a leader, even your accidental actions set the culture.

Walking the talk may be the most difficult skill to get right. Nobody ever does it 100 percent. Even Louverture came up short. To convince slaves to join the revolution, he told them he was working on behalf of Louis XVI. He wasn't. But without that lie the revolution might never have happened. Should he have risked the revolution to preserve his culture? What would be the point of that? He'd have ended up being able to console himself with having created a pure and perfect culture as he and his fellow mutineers were being executed.

When I was CEO of LoudCloud, I tried to create a transparent culture where we shared everything important with everyone. This led to a broad sense of ownership and enabled us to get more brains working on the biggest problems.

But after the dot-com crash in 2000, nobody trusted startups with their business anymore, and LoudCloud was suddenly headed for bankruptcy. I had a slim chance to move us into the software business, which would require less capital and give us a much better chance for survival. I told almost no one of my plans. Why? Because if word got out about the impending transformation not only would our current business fall apart, but so would the deal to enable the new business. When the truth ultimately emerged, as I sold LoudCloud and repurposed the remainder of the company into Opsware, our culture took a real hit. People trusted me a whole lot less. But I had to hurt the culture—to stop walking my own talk, for a time—to save the company.

Resuscitating our culture afterward wasn't easy. My approach was to admit all the sins of the past and reset us with a new level of transparency in the most memorable setting I could afford, which wasn't much. I scheduled an all-company off-site in Santa Cruz, California, and rented rooms in the Dream Inn, a motel. The catered meals were ham-salad sandwiches with drink coupons. I made everyone double up in the rooms, ostensibly to save even more money. The real reason was that sharing rooms was almost unheard-of for Silicon Valley technology companies and I wanted them to remember everything about the off-site. (The ploy backfired on me as I ended up rooming with my chief financial officer, Dave Conte, a heavy snorer.)

I made it clear that no work would occur the first afternoon and evening. We were to spend that time getting to know each other. That might seem redundant for a three-and-a-half-year-old company, but the idea was to begin to feel comfortable around one another again—a big ask.

The next day, I opened the meeting by saying, "Okay, I am the one who drove the last business into a ditch, so why should you trust me this time?" Then I had my management team present every aspect of the business, including the financials—especially the financials, down to every penny we had in the bank and all the debt—and the complete product and business strategy. Full transparency again, after a period of necessary obfuscation.

It mostly worked. Of the eighty people who attended the off-site, all but four stayed with the company through our ultimate sale to Hewlett-Packard five years later. I definitely did not walk the talk on our pivot, but thankfully I didn't trip and land face-first on the pavement, either.

MAKE ETHICS EXPLICIT

Uber has received a ton of publicity for having a totally broken culture, so you may be surprised to learn that Travis Kalanick designed its culture with great intention and programmed it into his organization with meticulous care. Uber's culture actually worked exactly as designed—only it had a serious design flaw.

Take a look at Uber's highly original cultural code, the values Kalanick laid down after he founded the company in 2009. Proud Uber employees circulated them widely:

1. Uber Mission
2. Celebrate Cities
3. Meritocracy and Toe-Stepping
4. Principled Confrontation
5. Winning: Champion's Mindset
6. Let Builders Build
7. Always Be Hustlin'
8. Customer Obsession
9. Make Big, Bold Bets
10. Make Magic
11. Be an Owner, not a Renter
12. Be Yourself
13. Optimistic Leadership
14. The Best Idea Wins

Kalanick also defined eight qualities he sought in his employees:

1. Vision
2. Quality Obsession
3. Innovation
4. Fierceness

5. Execution
6. Scale
7. Communication
8. Super Pumpedness

These are not run-of-the-mill values you'd pull out of a standard management book. Nor are they vague aspirations that would emerge from a consensus-building session off-site. These are values you get when a leader clearly communicates the behavior he wants.

If he put that much effort into Uber's culture, where did it go wrong? The problem was that the mind-set implicit in such values as *Meritocracy and Toe-Stepping, Winning: Champions Mindset, Always Be Hustlin'*, and *The Best Idea Wins* elevated one value above all: competitiveness. Kalanick was one of the most competitive people in the world and he drove that ethos into his company in every way possible. And it worked: by 2016, the company was valued at $66 billion.

The trainers at Uberversity, where new employees underwent a three-day initiation, began schooling everyone on this scenario: a rival company is launching a carpooling service in four weeks. It's impossible for Uber to beat them to market with a reliable carpool service of its own. What should the company do? The correct answer at Uberversity—and what Uber actually did when it learned about Lyft Line—was "Rig up a makeshift solution that we pretend is totally ready to go so we can beat the competitor to market." (Andreessen Horowitz, the venture capital firm where I work, invested in Lyft and I am on its board, so I was keenly aware of the dynamic between the companies—and I am decidedly biased.) Those, including the company's legal team, who proposed taking the time to come up with a workable product, one far better than Uber Pool 1.0, were told "That's not the Uber way." The underlying message was clear: if the choice is integrity or winning, at Uber we do whatever we have to do to win.

This competitiveness issue also came up when Uber began to challenge Didi Chuxing, the Chinese market leader in ride-sharing. To counter Uber, Didi employed very aggressive techniques including hacking Uber's app to send it fake riders. The Chinese law on the tactic wasn't entirely clear. The Chinese branch of Uber countered by hacking Didi right back. Uber then brought those techniques home to the United States by hacking Lyft with a program known as Hell, which inserted fake riders into Lyft's system while simultaneously funneling Uber the information it needed to recruit Lyft drivers. Did Kalanick instruct his subordinates to employ these measures, which were at best anticompetitive and at worst arguably illegal? It's difficult to say, but the point is that he didn't have to—he had already programmed the culture that engendered those measures.

When news leaked that the autonomous car unit at Alphabet's Waymo division was developing a ride-sharing app, Uber began aggressively recruiting Waymo's engineers to jump-start its own autonomous car effort. It did this despite the fact that Alphabet's subsidiary, Google, was a large investor in Uber, and the fact that David

Drummond, Alphabet's chief of legal and corporate development, sat on Uber's board. Kalanick even went as far as to buy a Waymo spinoff called Otto, which had allegedly stolen Waymo's intellectual property. Did Uber execs know that Otto possessed stolen IP? I can't say for sure, but it would have been culturally consistent.

Uber's cultural issues became visible to the world after a young woman named Susan Fowler joined the company as a site-reliability engineer in 2015. Fowler had a degree in physics and had written a book on microservices; she was brilliant and optimistic. But after completing Uber's training program, she swiftly experienced the culture's dark side. As she later wrote in a blog post that shook the company:

> After the first couple of weeks of training, I chose to join the team that worked on my area of expertise, and this is where things started getting weird. On my first official day rotating on the team, my new manager sent me a string of messages over company chat. He was in an open relationship, he said, and his girlfriend was having an easy time finding new partners but he wasn't. He was trying to stay out of trouble at work, he said, but he couldn't help getting in trouble, because he was looking for women to have sex with. It was clear that he was trying to get me to have sex with him, and it was so clearly out of line that I immediately took screenshots of these chat messages and reported him to HR.
>
> Uber was a pretty good-sized company at that time, and I had pretty standard expectations of how they

would handle situations like this. I expected that I would report him to HR, they would handle the situation appropriately, and then life would go on—unfortunately, things played out quite a bit differently. When I reported the situation, I was told by both HR and upper management that even though this was clearly sexual harassment and he was propositioning me, it was this man's first offense, and that they wouldn't feel comfortable giving him anything other than a warning and a stern talking-to. Upper management told me that he "was a high performer" (i.e. had stellar performance reviews from his superiors) and they wouldn't feel comfortable punishing him for what was probably just an innocent mistake on his part.

According to federal law, if a company receives a harassment complaint of any kind (it need not even be documented as Fowler's was), it must formally investigate it. Grasping this law is as basic to being an HR professional as grasping revenue recognition is to being an accountant. So why would the HR person at Uber knowingly commit a crime? Because the HR manager believed that disciplining a high-performing manager would be "uncompetitive."

There is zero chance that Kalanick thought it was a good idea not to investigate an HR complaint from a promising engineer. That was not the culture he'd intended to construct. Nowhere in his set of values did it say that it was okay for managers to sexually harass their employees. Nowhere was it implied. In fact, by all ac-

counts Kalanick was furious about the incident, which
he saw as a woman being judged on issues other than
performance. That, of course, was the opposite of "Best
Idea Wins." Somehow his culture was having a weird
counterproductive side effect.

The side effect continued to manifest itself. When an
Uber driver allegedly raped a passenger in India, execs
back home suspected the company's Indian rival Ola of
paying the passenger to fake her own rape. An enterpris-
ing Uber executive, Eric Alexander, took the initiative to
acquire the alleged victim's medical records as a way to
try to confirm this suspicion. When the news of this
maneuver became public, the world was outraged. Was
Uber bribing foreign officials to acquire the medical records of rape victims? What on earth was going on?

Once the heat came down, even his own board members turned on Kalanick. They were shocked, shocked
that there was gambling in the casino. Was the board
aware the entire time of the corporate value "Always
Be Hustlin'"? One hundred percent they were. Did
they know what it meant? If they did not, they were
negligent. I doubt they were negligent. There were many
stories over the years indicating which way the company would go if a law that it didn't like hampered its
competitiveness.

Was the board furious at Kalanick for designing such
an aggressive culture? On the contrary, they were thrilled
as long as he was making them billions. They were only
furious once he got caught—that is, once the flaws in the
culture became widely known outside the company.

From Kalanick's perspective, he had made his priorities crystal clear and the board had signed off on them for years. Openly proud of how he ran Uber, he loved its reputation for being the most competitive company in Silicon Valley. He believed and likely still believes that he did the right thing the entire way and furthermore exercised proper corporate governance as he made his beliefs clear to the board. Nobody can point to a decision that he made to enable sexual harassment, acquire medical records of rape victims, or any of the other transgressions.

That's the nature of culture. It's not a single decision—it's a code that manifests itself as a vast set of actions taken over time. No one person makes or takes all these actions. Cultural design is a way to program the actions of an organization, but, like computer programs, every culture has bugs. And cultures are significantly more difficult to debug than programs.

Kalanick didn't intend to build an unethical organization, just a hypercompetitive one. But he had bugs in his code.

Huawei, China's telecom-equipment giant, had a similarly meteoric rise fueled by a powerful but buggy "wolf culture." These transgressions led to lawsuits, charges of international bribery, and recently the arrest of its CFO for bank fraud.

It all began with tenacity and competitiveness. As the *New York Times* reported, employees were given mattresses so they could nap as they worked late nights, and were onboarded in a boot-camp-style training course that entailed morning jogs and the performance of skits about how they'd help customers even in dangerous war zones.

Employees were also required to study and sign a set of business guidelines each year. More informally—which is where culture lives—there were "red lines" they were told never to cross: disclosing company secrets or breaking laws and sanctions. "Yellow line" situations, however, were a gray area. Workers were essentially encouraged to ignore rules about using gifts or other inducements to win customers. This led to bribery allegations in Ghana and Algeria, to sanction-busting behavior in Iran, and to Huawei's acknowledgment that an employee had stolen the software underlying T-Mobile's smartphone-testing robot, Tappy—and even the end of Tappy's arm, which he slipped into his laptop bag—to help Huawei produce its own robot. It led, in other words, to red-line violations.

In a 2015 corporate amnesty, thousands of Huawei employees admitted to transgressions ranging from bribery to fraud—perhaps, CEO Ren Zhengfei acknowledged, because the company used to evaluate staff solely according to how much business they won. Even after the seemingly shocking results of the amnesty program, Ren emailed everyone to say that adherence to ethical standards was important, of course, but "if it blocks the business from producing grain, then we all starve to death." (You could argue, of course, that if Huawei was doing the bidding of the Chinese government—breaking the rules as a matter of national policy, the way an intelligence agency would—then its culture was doing exactly what it was supposed to.)

What you measure is what you value. Huawei's results

echoed Uber's. Once you remove the requirement to follow certain rules or obey certain laws, you basically remove ethics from the culture.

It's impossible to design a bug-free culture. But it's vital to understand that the most dangerous bugs are the ones that cause ethical breaches. This is why Louverture emphasized ethics so explicitly. Spelling out what your organization must never do is the best way to inoculate yourself against bugs that cause ethical breaches.

Recall Louverture's speech to his soldiers: "Do not disappoint me . . . do not permit the desire for booty to turn you aside . . . it will be time enough to think of material things when we have driven the enemy from our shores." Consider how strange this statement must have seemed. Louverture's highest goal, like Uber's, was winning. If he didn't win the war, slavery would not be abolished. Nothing could be more important than this, could it? If it made his soldiers happy to pillage, why disallow it?

As Louverture explained, "We are fighting that liberty—the most precious of earthly possessions—may not perish." When it comes to ethics, you have to explain the "why." Why can't you pillage? Because pillaging would corrupt the real goal, which isn't winning, but liberty. In other words, if you win in the wrong way, what do you actually win? If you fight in a manner that strips liberty from bystanders, how will you ever build a free society? And if you don't build a free society, what are you fighting for? Louverture treated an army of illiterate former slaves as if they were philosophers, and they rose to the challenge.

After Uber's board ousted Kalanick and brought in a new CEO, Dara Khosrowshahi, Khosrowshahi immediately replaced the offending cultural values with the following new ones:

We build globally, we live locally.
We are customer obsessed.
We celebrate differences.
We act like owners.
We persevere.
We value ideas over hierarchy.
We make big bold bets.
We do the right thing. Period.

The key one was "We do the right thing. Period."

Kalanick's code was dangerous but unique—only Uber had it. The new values are safer—but they could be anyone's.

Look again at the new code's ethical injunction: *We do the right thing. Period.* Khosrowshahi is a strong CEO and likely has a comprehensive plan to program his values into the culture. But when we compare his precept to Louverture's, there's a clear gap in precision.

1. What, exactly, does "Do the right thing" mean?
2. And how does "Period" clarify that?

Does "Do the right thing" mean make the quarter or tell the truth? Does it mean use your judgment or obey the law? Does it mean you can excuse losses by claiming some moral imperative? Will employees who are hired from a culture like Facebook have a different view of "Do the right thing" than employees hired from Oracle?

Louverture spelled out what "Do the right thing" meant: don't pillage, don't cheat on your wife, take responsibility for yourself, personal industry, social morality, public education, religious toleration, free trade, civic pride, racial equality, and on and on. His instructions were specific, emphatic, and unceasing.

It's also critical that leaders emphasize the "why" behind their values every chance they get, because the "why" is what gets remembered. The "what" is just another item in a giant stack of things you are supposed to do. So for Uber to merely say *We do what's right, period,* means the company missed a big opportunity.

Finally, "Do the right thing. Period," makes the issue seem simple, and therefore trivial. But ethics is not easy; it's complex. That's why Louverture spoke to his slave army as though they were philosophers. He needed them to understand that they would have to think deeply about their choices.

If you remember one thing, remember that ethics are about hard choices. Do you tell a little white lie to investors or do you lay off a third of the company? Do you get publicly embarrassed by a competitor or do you deceive a customer? Do you deny someone a raise that they need or do you make your company a little less fair?

No matter how difficult such questions seem, your task will never be as challenging as implanting ethics in a slave army during a war.

3 THE WAY OF THE WARRIOR

The shit I kick, ripping through the vest
Biggie Smalls passing any test
I'm ready to die.
—*Notorious B.I.G.*

The samurai, the warrior class of ancient Japan, had a powerful code we call "bushido," or "the way of the warrior." This code enabled the samurai to rule Japan from 1186 until 1868—nearly seven hundred years—and their beliefs endured long after their reign. The samurai are the taproot of Japanese culture to this day.

Some of bushido's tenets, selected from Shintoism, Buddhism, and Confucianism, are thousands of years old, so portions of its playbook seem antiquated. Yet the culture persevered for so astonishingly long because it provided a framework for handling every situation or ethical dilemma you might come across. Bushido's dictates were crisp, coherent, and comprehensive. The samurai's meticulous approach to building a 360-degree culture is extraordinarily applicable today.

WHAT DID CULTURE MEAN TO THE SAMURAI?

Bushido looks like a set of principles, but it's a set of practices. The samurai defined culture as a code of action, a system not of values but of virtues. A value is merely a belief, but a virtue is a belief that you actively pursue or embody. The reason so many efforts to establish "corporate values" are basically worthless is that they emphasize beliefs instead of actions. Culturally, what you believe means nearly nothing. What you *do* is who you are.

Even the samurai oath is oriented toward action:

> I will never fall behind others in pursuing the way of
> the warrior.
> I will always be ready to serve my lord.
> I will honor my parents.
> I will serve compassionately for the benefit of others.

Hagakure, the most famous collection of samurai wisdom, instructs: "The extent of one's courage or cowardice cannot be measured in ordinary times. All is revealed when something happens."

THE IMPORTANCE OF DEATH

A striking aspect of modern Japanese culture is the craftsmanship and attention to detail. From sushi makers to whiskey distillers to Kobe beef producers to car manufacturers, the Japanese focus on quality, and their proficiency in attaining it, is remarkable. Where did this culture of carefulness originate?

It began with death. The most famous line in *Hagakure* is "The way of the warrior is to be found in dying." Another crucial text, *Bushido Shoshinshu*, opens with one of the most shocking rules in any culture: "Keep death in mind at all times." Of all the aspects of life you might want to meditate on constantly, death would seem like the last one on the list. Before studying the bushido, I would rather have watched Hillary Clinton and Donald Trump take each other on in a ten-hour dance competition than contemplate death.

Bushido Shoshinshu explains the idea behind that contemplation:

> *If you realize that the life that is here today is not certain on the morrow, then when you take your orders from your employer, and when you look in on your parents, you will have the sense that this may be the last time—so you cannot fail to become truly attentive to your employer and your parents.*

The text takes pains to describe what the concept *doesn't* mean. It doesn't mean just sitting around waiting to die:

> *If you face death in that way, loyalty and familial duty to your employer and parents will be neglected, and your professional warriorhood will wind up defective. This will never do.*

The idea is to take care of your public and private duties day and night, and then whenever you have free time when your mind is unoccupied, you think of death, bringing it to mind attentively.

This rule was the foundation of the culture. Note how awareness of mortality underpinned both loyalty and scrupulous attention to detail. From *Hagakure*:

Every morning, samurai would diligently groom themselves by bathing in the open air, shaving their foreheads, putting fragrant oil in their hair, cutting their fingernails and filing them with pumice stone, then polishing them with wood sorrel. Of course, military equipment was kept neat, dusted, and oiled to be free of rust. Although paying so much attention to personal appearance may seem vain, it is because of the samurai's resolve to die at any moment that he makes preparations so meticulously. If slain with an unkempt appearance, he will be scorned by his enemy as being unclean.

A warrior known as the Master Archer had a sign on his wall to remind him that he must be "Always on the Battlefield." Devoted warriors would even wear a wooden sword to the bath, to keep themselves ever mindful of combat, readiness, and the potential for death.

The biggest threat to your company's culture is a time of crisis, a period when you're getting crushed by the competition or are nearing bankruptcy. How do you focus on the task at hand if you might be killed at any moment? The answer: they can't kill you if you're already dead. If you've already accepted the worst possible outcome, you have nothing to lose. *Hagakure* commands you to imagine and accept the worst in gory detail:

> *Begin each day pondering death as its climax. Each morning, with a calm mind, conjure images in your head of your last moments. See yourself being pierced by bow and arrow, gun, sword, or spear, or being swept away by a giant wave, vaulting into a fiery inferno, taking a lightning strike, being shaken to death in a great earthquake, falling hundreds of feet from a high cliff top, succumbing to a terminal illness, or just dropping dead unexpectedly. Every morning, be sure to meditate yourself into a trance of death.*

Meditating on your company's downfall will enable you to build your culture the right way. Imagine you've gone bankrupt. Were you a great place to work? What was it like to do business with you? Did your encounters with people leave them better off or worse off? Did the quality of your products make you proud?

Modern companies tend to focus on metrics like goals, missions, and quarterly numbers. They rarely ask why all their employees come to work every day. Is it for the money? What's more valuable, the money or the time? My mentor, Bill Campbell, used to say, "We are doing it for each other. How much do you care about the people you're working with? Do you want to let them down?"

Whether your aim is to keep death in mind, to do it for each other, or some analogous formulation, the glue that binds a company culture is that the work must be meaningful for its own sake.

DEFINING THE VIRTUES

The samurai code rested on eight virtues: Rectitude or justice, courage, honor, loyalty, benevolence, politeness, self-control, and veracity or sincerity. Each virtue was carefully defined and then reinforced through a set of principles, practices, and stories. They all worked together as a system, balancing one another in a way that made it very difficult for any individual virtue to be misunderstood or misused. Let's zoom in on the virtues of honor, politeness, and veracity or sincerity to see how this works.

Honor

The samurai regarded honor as the immortal part of themselves. Without honor, every other virtue was worthless and bestial. The samurai took this idea to extremes that we would find, well, extreme. There is a famous story about a well-meaning citizen who called the attention of a samurai to a flea on his back, and was promptly cut in two for his pains. As fleas were parasites that fed on animals, the citizen had publicly identified the samurai as a beast, which was unpardonable.

While I have sometimes thought about cutting someone in half for questioning my integrity in a meeting, that generally wouldn't work in today's world. But your individual reputation and honor should mean something within your company, and be at stake in everything you do. Does the integrity of that deal meet your standard? Does the quality of your team's work measure up? Are you willing to put your name on it? If the customer or your competitor questions your behavior, are you comfortable knowing that you acted with honor?

Still, if you could be summarily executed for a faux pas, that's a problem. There had to be a complementary part of the culture that ordained how you should behave in all situations to avoid this kind of sudden death. Enter *politeness*.

Politeness

The politeness virtue consisted of a complex set of rules that determined how the samurai should behave in all situations—how he must bow, how he must walk and sit, even how he must drink tea.

Though the specific rules may seem arbitrary, they were rooted in the belief that politeness is the most profound way to express love and respect for others. It wasn't just rule-following, but a gateway to deeper intimacy.

Bushido, Soul of Japan gives us an idea of how this concept still works in Japan:

> *You are out in the hot, glaring sun with no shade over you; a Japanese acquaintance passes you by; you accost him, and instantly his hat is off—well, that is perfectly natural, but the "awfully funny" perfor-*

mance is, that all the while he talks with you his para-
sol is down and he stands in the glaring sun also. How
foolish!—Yes, exactly so, provided the motive were less
than this: "You are in the sun; I sympathise with you;
I would willingly take you under my parasol if it were
large enough, or if we were familiarly acquainted; as I
cannot shade you, I will share your discomforts."

In the United States today, we get on Twitter and decry the lack of empathy in our country—and then we wonder why empathy keeps diminishing. A culture is not the sum of its outrage; it's a set of actions. In a competitive corporate world, politeness might seem like a throwaway virtue. In fact, the way the samurai took the action-oriented nature of politeness and used it to express the abstract concepts of love and respect is exceptionally instructive.

But how did the samurai get around the issue of being fake? How did they stop people from using politeness to feign respect, thereby creating a culture premised on duplicity? Again, their system came into play. The samurai combined the virtue of *politeness* with the virtue of *veracity or sincerity.* Specifically, they defined politeness without veracity as an empty gesture. Lying to be polite is politeness without form and has no value.

Veracity or Sincerity

The samurai notion of sincerity was influenced by Confucius, who wrote: "Sincerity is the end and the beginning of all things; without Sincerity there would be nothing."

The culture of veracity was so strong that a samurai's

word was considered the truth and written agreements were deemed unnecessary. This was reinforced in parenting, where children were raised on stories of being put to death for lying. Words were seen as sacred.

This passage about Hiko'uemon, a samurai in the 1600s, illustrates the virtue:

> When Moro'oka Hiko'uemon was summoned, he was told to sign an oath to the deities that his testimony was true. "A samurai's word is harder than metal. Once I have decided something, not even the gods can change it." Consequently, he did not have to make an oath.

APPLYING THE METHOD

When we started Andreessen Horowitz in 2009, the one virtue I knew I wanted in our culture was *respect for the entrepreneur*. Venture capitalists (VCs) depend on entrepreneurs for their existence, and I wanted our culture to reflect that. The systemic problem was that as entrepreneurs asked venture capitalists for funding, VCs tended to see themselves as in the commanding role. Many carried themselves accordingly.

I took a samurai-style approach. First, we defined the virtue thoroughly, taking pains to note what it did not mean:

We respect the intense struggle of the entrepreneurial process and we know that without the entrepreneurs we have no business. *When dealing with entrepreneurs, we always show up* *on time and we always get back to them timely and with substantive feedback, even if it's bad news (like a rejection). We have an optimistic view of the future and believe that entrepreneurs, whether they succeed or fail, are working to help us achieve a better future. As a result, we never publicly criticize any entrepreneur or startup (doing so is a fireable offense).*

This does not mean that we leave CEOs in place forever. Our obligation is to the company not the founder. If the founder is no longer capable of running the company, the founder will not remain as CEO.

Yet there was still an opportunity for people to misinterpret this virtue as "never saying anything negative to an entrepreneur," so we paired it with another virtue:

We tell the truth even if it hurts. *When talking to an entrepreneur, an LP [limited partner], a partner, or each other, we strive to tell the truth. We are open and honest. We do not withhold material information or tell half truths. Even if the truth will be difficult to hear or to say, we err on the side of truth in the face of difficult consequences.*

We do not, however, dwell on trivial truths with the intention of hurting people's feelings or making them look bad. We tell the truth to make people better not worse.

To cement this practice in our culture, we focused not on the value of respect, but on the virtue of being on time. If you were late for a meeting with an entrepreneur, you had to pay a fine of ten dollars per minute. Avoiding the fine took practice and hard work, and embedded a number of great habits into our culture. You had to plan your previous meeting correctly, so it wouldn't conflict with the meeting with the entrepreneur. You not only had to end that meeting with discipline, but you had to run it with discipline, so everything got done in the time allotted. You had to avoid being distracted by random texts or emails. You even had to think about when to go to the restroom.

We didn't collect much in fines—less than one thousand dollars, most of it early on—because the threat of the fine made everyone constantly aware of being punctual and of the respect owed the entrepreneur.

Other VCs as well as the people covering the industry misinterpreted the virtue and referred to it as "founder friendly," a massive corruption of the concept that has delivered us a competitive advantage for years. Being "founder friendly" implies that you take the founder's side even when he is mistaken. This kind of "virtue" helps nobody. In fact, it creates a culture of lies. Any time you decide one group is inherently good or bad regardless of their behavior, you program dishonesty into your organization.

MAKING THE CULTURE LAST

In America, parents have trouble convincing their children to stay polite for a single dinner party. How did the entire country of Japan embrace politeness for more than ten centuries? It helped that the samurai required everyone to study the code, commit it to memory, and live it every day—but other cultures have required that kind of study, and they didn't last nearly as long. The samurai endured because of two additional techniques. First, they detailed every permutation of potential cultural or ethical dilemmas to prevent the code from being misinterpreted or deliberately misused. Second, they stamped their code deep with vivid stories.

A hallmark of the code was its detailed consideration of potential circumstances. Recall Uber's terse "We do the right thing. Period." Now consider the *Bushido Shoshinshu*:

> *There are three ways of doing right.*
>
> *Suppose you are going somewhere with an acquaintance who has a hundred ounces of gold and wants to leave it at your house until returning, instead of taking the trouble to carry it with him. Suppose you take the gold and put it away where no one can find it. Now suppose your companion dies during the trip, perhaps from food poisoning or stroke. No one else knows he left gold at your house, and no else knows you have it.*
>
> *Under these circumstances, if you have no thought but of sorrow for the tragedy, and you report the gold to the relatives of the deceased, sending it to them as soon as possible, then you can truly be said to have done right.*
>
> *Now suppose the man with the gold was just an acquaintance, not such a close friend. No one knows about the gold he left with you, so there will be no in-*

quiries. You happen to be in tight circumstances at the moment, so this is a bit of luck; why not just keep quiet about it?

If you are ashamed to find such thoughts occurring to you, and so you change your mind and return the gold to the rightful heirs, you could be said to have done right out of a sense of shame.

Now suppose someone in your household—maybe your wife, your children, or your servants—knows about the gold. Suppose you return the gold to the legitimate heirs out of shame for any designs anyone in your household might conceive, and out of fear for the legal consequences. Then you should be said to do right out of shame in relation to others.

But what would you do if no one knew about it at all?

The story makes no ultimate distinction between doing right for "the right reasons" or out of shame or guilt. *Why* you do right is not important. Doing right is all that counts. But the people who created the code understood that doing right is harder in some circumstances than others, so they provided case studies.

Will you do the right thing only if you risk getting caught for not doing it? How about if you don't really risk getting caught? How about if you know nobody will know, nobody will miss getting the money, you don't have a relationship with the person, and you really need the money? That last scenario is particularly challenging. If you don't clarify exactly what "the right thing" is for a tough call like that, it won't be totally clear what your employees should do when they come to one—and tough calls are what define a company and a culture.

STORIES

You can read all you want to about the virtue of loyalty, but one vivid story from *Hagakure* brings it to life:

> *The family history of Lord Soma is recorded in a scroll called the* Chiken Marokashi. *It was an unequaled family genealogy in Japan. The lord's mansion suddenly caught fire one year. Lord Soma lamented: "I do not bemoan the loss of the manor and its fittings. They can all be replaced if they are destroyed in the fire. Regrettably, though, I couldn't retrieve our treasured heirloom, the family tree."*
>
> *One of his attendants declared: "I shall enter the flames and save this treasure." Lord Soma and the other retainers chortled incredulously, "How can you salvage it now when the building is engulfed by this fire?" The retainer was never effusive in service, nor had he ever been exceptionally useful, but for some reason his lord was fond of him as he was diligent. "By no means have I been an effective servant to His Lordship because of my clumsiness. Nevertheless, I have always been ready to sacrifice my life for something useful should the opportunity arise. I believe that time is now." With that, he stormed into the blazing inferno.*
>
> *As soon as the fire had been put out, Lord Soma instructed his men, "Find his body. It is such a shame!"*

*They searched through the burnt ruins and finally lo-
cated his charred remains in the garden area next to
the residence. Blood gushed from his stomach as they
turned his prostrated body over. Evidently he had slit
open his belly and inserted the document inside, protecting it from the flames. Henceforth, it became known
as the* Chi-keizu *or "Blood Genealogy."*

Telling this story was a nearly perfect way to embed
loyalty. The retainer was a mediocre person leading a
mediocre life, but with one heroic act, he became immortal. How can anyone forget him carving a hole in himself
to save the scroll? Let alone the ringing name given the
document he preserved: *Blood Genealogy.*

Stories and sayings define cultures. John Morgridge,
the CEO of Cisco from 1988 to 1995, wanted every spare
nickel spent on the business. But as many of his employees had come from free-spending cultures, simply
reminding them to be frugal didn't get his point across.
Morgridge walked the talk by staying at the Red Roof Inn,
but even his example didn't prove truly contagious. So he
came up with a pithy axiom: "If you cannot see your car
from your hotel room, then you are paying too much."
When his top executives heard that, they understood that
business-class tickets and fancy dinners were out of the
question. More subtly—but even more crucially—they
understood that the point of business travel was to meet
customer needs, not to enjoy perks.

When I was at Netscape Communications in the early
days, we operated like a debate club. A debate club where

everyone wanted to weigh in on every decision and then, if they lost, to revisit the decision as often as possible. We couldn't get any work done because we were unwilling to commit the flag and move on.

When Jim Barksdale became the company's CEO in 1995, he knew he had to change that culture. But how? Create a cultural value telling people to disagree and commit? While *disagree and commit* is a great decision-making rule, as I'll discuss later, it's not easy to insert it into a culture accustomed to doing the opposite. Imagine being in a heated debate and hearing someone say, "Let's disagree and commit." You'd respond, "Commit to what? My idea or yours?"

So what did Barksdale do? He created a piece of lore so memorable it outlived the company itself. At a company all-hands he said:

> We have three rules here at Netscape. The first rule is if you see a snake, don't call committees, don't call your buddies, don't form a team, don't get a meeting together, just kill the snake.
>
> The second rule is don't go back and play with dead snakes. Too many people waste too much time on decisions that have already been made.
>
> And the third rule of snakes is: all opportunities start out looking like snakes.

That story was so clear and so funny that nearly everyone got the point immediately. If you didn't, everyone else was very excited to retell you the story. We told the story over and over again and the company changed. Once people realized that killing the snake was much more important than how we killed it, our new culture unleashed a flurry of creative energy. As the company bringing the Internet to life, we faced many snakes. The Internet had no security, so we invented Secure Sockets Layer (SSL). The Internet had no way of maintaining browser state between sessions, so we invented cookies. The Internet couldn't be programmed easily, so we invented JavaScript. Were these the optimal solutions? Probably not. But those snakes died fast, we never played with them again, and the technologies we created still dominate the Internet.

Why did the bushido have such a profound impact on Japanese society? The complex answer is that the samurai developed and refined their culture continuously over a very long period of time, using a variety of psychologically sophisticated techniques to make it feel indelible, inescapable, and completely natural.

The simple answer is that they kept death in mind at all times.

4 THE WARRIOR OF A DIFFERENT WAY: THE STORY OF SHAKA SENGHOR

Let a n*gg* try me, try me
I'ma get his whole mutherfuckin' family
And I ain't playin' with nobody
Fuck around and I'ma catch a body
—*Dej Loaf*

Shaka Senghor did not grow up in ancient Japan, but perhaps he should have. Philosophical, highly disciplined, and ferocious when he has to be, he would have been well suited to samurai life. But he grew up in inner-city Detroit and became a warrior of a different way.

I first met Senghor in 2015 through an unusual set of circumstances. I was scheduled to interview Oprah Winfrey after Andreessen Horowitz screened her new OWN show *Belief*. Interviewing arguably the best interviewer of my generation was more than a little intimidating. It felt like I had to give Albert Einstein a pop quiz on the special theory of relativity. I asked Oprah if she wouldn't mind riding with me to the interview, so that she could school me on the art of drawing people out and help me avoid total embarrassment.

In the car, she said, "The first thing you need to know is that you cannot work off a list of questions, because if you do you won't listen and you will miss the most important question: the follow-up question." A great point, but one I already understood. I said, "I need to know how you ask people really aggressive questions and, instead of getting defensive, they open up and start crying." She said:

> Well, before I interview anyone I start by asking what their intentions are and I say, "I will help you get those intentions, but you have to trust me." I'll give you an example. Last week I was filming my show Super Soul Sunday and I had this guest on, Shaka Senghor, who had just spent nineteen years in prison, seven in solitary confinement for a murder he did commit. He had big muscles, dreadlocks, tattoos, and looked very scary. I asked him what his intentions were and he said, "It's my intention to let people know that you shouldn't be defined by the very worst thing that you have ever done in your life. People can be redeemed." I said, "I got it and will help you get it, but you have to trust me."
>
> So we start filming and I ask him, "When did you turn to crime?" He said, "I hit the streets when I was fourteen years old." But I had read his book. So I said, "What

about that time when you were nine years old and you came home with a perfect report card and your mother threw a pot at your head? How did that make you feel?" His body language closed up and he said, "It didn't feel very good." So I said, "You have to trust me. How did it make you feel?" He said, "It made me feel like nothing that I would do in life would ever matter." I said: "You didn't hit the streets when you were fourteen. You hit the streets when you were nine." And we both started crying.

That was about the most incredible story I had ever heard, so I immediately told it to my wife, Felicia. This may have been a mistake. My wife is both the biggest Oprah fan in the world and literally Miss Congeniality (she won that award in the Sugar Ray Robinson Youth Contest). A week later she told me, "I reached out to Shaka on Facebook and we're now Facebook friends." I replied, "Did you hear the whole story? He just spent nineteen years in prison for a murder he *did* commit. That's not a guy that you just friend on Facebook!" She said, "Well, he's going to be in town, so I invited him out to dinner." Uh-oh.

I made a reservation at John Bentley's, two blocks from my house. If anything went wrong, I figured we could make a fast getaway. Instead, after a three-hour dinner, I invited Shaka back to our house, where we talked for another five hours.

He was maybe the most insightful person I had ever spoken to about how to build a culture and run an organization.

He had been the CEO of a prison gang, a tough organization to manage. (His group and rival prison organizations did not self-identify as gangs, but as religious organizations. I will refer to them as squads.) And he not only built a strong culture—he then changed his squad into something entirely different. He displayed all the skills this book hopes to impart: he shaped a culture, recognized its flaws, then transformed it into something better.

Another factor that made me want to write about Senghor is that people who end up in prison generally come from broken cultures. Their parents abandoned or beat them. Their friends sold them out. And they can't rely on a common understanding of basic ideas like keeping your word. Prison provides culture's hardest test case; to build culture there, you have to start from the very beginning, from first principles.

CULTURAL ORIENTATION

James White (Senghor's birth name) went to prison at an age when most of us went to college. College culture introduced most of us to frat parties; prison culture introduced White to extreme violence and intimidation. As he told me, when he went to prison he believed it would be his home from then on.

Going into prison at nineteen and knowing that I was about to serve this long sentence, I couldn't see two decades out. I felt this was forever. The only thing that was guaranteed was the end of my sentence, forty years off. The idea of getting out at sixty was ridiculous.

First came county jail. A couple of things were happening when you arrived. One, guys were trying to identify if they had a beef with you from the streets. Two, they were trying to figure out if you could be exploited. Every tier had a Rock Boss or a crew that ran the tier. Outside your cell you walked into a little area called the Day Room, which had toilets, showers, and some community tables. Rock Bosses sat on the tables like lions looking for prey. A Rock Boss would be more chill than his second in command and his guys; if he was a lion, his guys were the hyenas.

One Rock Boss asked me, "Where are you from?" It was more of a diagnostic than a question. When I replied "Brightmo"—the 'hood pronunciation of Brightmoor, a neighborhood in Detroit—I gained credibility. Had I been from the suburbs, it would have indicated vulnerability. The next question was, "What you in here for?" I replied "Murder." Murder was a much more prestigious crime than, say, a sex offense, which would have made me a target.

So I was safe for the moment, but I could see everything going forward would be a test. If people were playing basketball and you said, "I got next," and then somebody else said they got next, you had to decide if you would let a motherfucker take your next or not. If not, you had to be willing to stand up for yourself and fight.

It's one integrated system from the streets to the jail

to the prison. Your personal brand follows you. Do peo-
ple know you from the streets as someone that's got
respect? Do you have dirt on your name for snitching?
There was this whole predatory energy. If family put
money on your books you can be robbed. You might be
vulnerable sexually.

It's literally all in the first day that this is what it is.
They called it the gladiator school, because it's where
you established your rank.

After he transferred to state prison, White faced an
even more intense version of orientation.

The new men were kept in quarantine for two weeks to
make sure we didn't have any diseases or other issues
that would keep us out of the general population. The
day we got out, we saw a guy get stabbed in the neck.
People get stabbed in areas of the prison where there
are no officers—on the back staircase; in the recreation
center where one officer watches three hundred men; in
the corridor to the chow hall or to the law library. So
we're in the recreation center and this guy gets stabbed
and the guy stabbing him does it so calmly and casually,
discards the knife, and goes to the chow hall.

Guys were visibly shaken, like, "Where the fuck are
we at?" I remember thinking, So this is the extreme
end of what happens in prison. And then asking my-
self, If you get into a conflict with somebody, could you
stab them and just keep it moving? I had never stabbed
anybody. I had shot someone, but that was a reaction

to a conflict on the streets. It was very different from premeditating, "Okay, I am going to stab this person. Where am I going to stab this person at? Do I want to scare him, wound him, get him to leave the yard I'm on, or kill him?" In prison you stab with many different intentions.

It takes callousness to do that, and I didn't have that yet. So I had to ask myself, If this is about survival, can you make that call? You don't know who the fuck you are in prison until you face something that makes you fearful or courageous. Some of the guys I thought were tough guys were really affected by the stabbing, but I realized that I wasn't. I was never an initiator of conflict, but I did grow up fighting and I was really good at it. If we were fighting I was like, "Let's get to it." I knew that if this was the worst, then I could make that decision and survive.

One violent object lesson, a moment of profound intro-spection, and White was fully oriented into Michigan's prison culture. He knew that to succeed there, he had to change—and he did.

WHITE'S RISE

White's prison was run by five gangs: the Sunni Muslims, the Nation of Islam, the Moorish Science Temple of America, the Five Percenters, and the Melanic Islamic Palace of the Rising Sun, known as the Melanics. The squads controlled commerce and provided their members with protection and amenities like drugs, cigarettes, and better food supplied by their friends in the kitchen, such as chicken or fresh ground beef. A new man who didn't join a gang was vulnerable.

White joined the Melanics, a squad that had originated in prison and taught idiosyncratic principles derived from the Black Panthers and Malcolm X, including self-determination and using education as a force for black uplift. The Melanics stood in contrast to the Nation of Islam, a chapter of the national organization, and the Sunni Muslims, who followed the Koran. (Unlike states such as California, where street gangs had chapters that ran prisons, most of the squads in the Michigan system were nominally organized around a form of worship.) The Melanics were relatively small, numbering about two hundred members, but they had a reputation for recruiting tough guys and running a tight ship. Yet White soon discovered that the gang wasn't living up to its code:

In prison, you have these very charismatic guys, great orators. They move their team into doing all kinds of shit using their charisma—but beneath it is no substance.

Our leaders were charismatic but duplicitous. For example, one of our guys was named T Man. He had money coming in from outside and people in our organization knew that, and knew that he was insecure about whether he was black or mixed race, so they were manipulating him and stealing his money. Uncertainty about which clique you were in made you vulnerable. I was like, "We're not doing that anymore, because it's against our code." The leaders weren't cool with that because they were profiting off this guy. So I said, "The people of this organization are going to ride with you or ride with me." The young guys wanted to ride with me, because they wanted to do the right thing. I was able to challenge the leadership with their own moral code.

In the Melanics, you couldn't run a straight coup and take over violently because part of our code was that you could never physically violate another member. So my takeover had to be psychological. I'd use the Socratic method at our meetings and ask the group questions such as "If a leader does not follow his own instructions, is he a leader?" Our members began to realize we needed to change, and they followed my idea that we're going to do what the fuck we say we're gonna do. As I rose to the top, the old leaders gradually became executive advisors. They still had privileges, but no direct control.

White began to understand that even observing the Melanics' code to the letter wasn't going to fully satisfy him.

I first realized that I could be a different person when I read The Autobiography of Malcolm X. *I saw that it was possible to change. But I also had to deal with the environment I was in. I had Malcolm X on one shoulder saying "You can be better" and the prison guy on the other shoulder saying "Fuck this motherfucker, he should have paid the three dollars when it was due." So*

I was a sophisticated thug. The clash of the two voices led me to develop a more diplomatic approach to conflict. I still made guys aware of the threat of violence, but also suggested we could resolve issues without stripping away your manhood.

It was at this point that I began to realize that everything that I came from on the streets was filled with bad energy and bad intentions, so I changed my name to James X. Everyone began calling me Jay X. But then, as I did research on Africa, I took the name Shaka Senghor, from the great warrior Shaka Zulu and from Léopold Senghor, the Senegalese poet and cultural theorist who served as the first president of Senegal.

When you have power, you have responsibility. It took me a long while to realize that the plays we were making affected not only me and my squad, but the whole prison environment. And that when a member left, he would carry that culture with him. First I had to learn there was a different way, then I had to master those skills, then I had to decide that was truly how I wanted to live my life. It was a three-step process, and it took me nine years to get through it. I was lucky it only took that long—due to my status, the other men didn't try to test me, so I didn't regress.

The Melanics' code was complex, but it essentially made everyone responsible for his fellow members. If an outsider struck a member, the entire organization would rise against him, which meant he would not be safe in any prison. You had to come to the aid of any member in need who was a worthy brother; his beef became your beef. If a member was deemed unworthy—often because he hadn't come to another member's aid—he lost his protection.

Senghor focused on the following principles: Never take advantage of members. Never physically accost them. And, in general, treat them the way you'd want to be treated.

Then he began to embed these principles in the squad:

You're dealing with low levels of literacy, so people memorized the code without understanding it. Because they didn't really understand it, they weren't living it.

To build the culture, we would hold study groups once or twice a week. As educational director, I'd pass out literature such as Visions for Black Men *by Na'im Akbar,* The Autobiography of Malcolm X, *James Allen's* As a Man Thinketh, *or Napoleon Hill's* Think and Grow Rich. *I wrote study guides that broke these books into basic components, and I made it mandatory for guys to study. Two years after joining up, I became the Melanics' cultural leader, which meant the leader. The younger guys really bonded to me, because everybody wants something to believe in.*

If you're not honoring the culture yourself, nobody fucking believes you. The principles were my natural principles. I believed in them. I was also willing to defend them. This shifted the culture to a better place.

Senghor explained how the idea of making the cultural principles universal worked:

Let's say this is our crew: me, you, and Cartheu. Cartheu decides to rob a motherfucker, and word comes back to us that that guy and his friends now want to fuck Cartheu up. So we have a conflict. Because in our code, we don't allow anyone to do anything to our members. But Cartheu has violated our tenet that you never compromise the organization by doing dumb shit. So we have a responsibility to protect him, we have a responsibility to protect the organization, and then we have an external responsibility to deal with the person who was robbed.

Poor leadership would say, "Let's get a couple of soldiers and go fuck these guys up," and then we'll deal with our guy internally. That was the culture when I came in. But that way of operating gives the other organization moral high ground—they can say we let our members do random bullshit. So I shifted our way so there was a consequence for Cartheu, not for the guy he robbed. Cartheu should apologize to him and pay restitution.

If you handle external matters this way, people in your organization will look at that as a model. If you don't, then the way you treat outsiders will leak back into your own organization.

THE TURNING POINT: UNINTENDED CONSEQUENCES

Senghor forced the Melanics to live up to their code, but that code was still largely the one he had inherited until a conflict with the Nation of Islam caused him to reconsider everything.

There were two schools of thought on how to organize your squad in the Michigan prison system. One system prevailed at Jackson State Prison, run by the older guys, and the other at Michigan Reformatory, run by us. At Jackson, the guys had access to hard drugs, which they used to incentivize addicts to take out their enemies. Their power derived from having so many hit men on payroll.

Our members weren't into heroin, so a business model based on addiction wasn't an option, but I don't think I would have used it in any case. That model, built on a foundation of payments and manipulation, led to a weak organization. Your team wasn't battle-ready, because it lacked what you need when things get difficult: loyalty and commitment.

I based our system in the Melanics on belonging and loyalty. It started with selection. I would be very clear that there were two requirements. You either had to be willing to serve a life sentence for whatever we asked you to do, or be willing to die.

Once in, in order to stay in, you had to carry yourself in a certain way. You couldn't use the N-word, or profanity. If you smoked, you couldn't smoke while wearing your membership badge. You couldn't get caught by the guards smoking weed or drinking prison wine, because this showed a lack of intelligence and self-control. You couldn't do anything that would be perceived as weak or disrespectful. Your shoes had to be clean and your prison blues had to be neat and pressed. In addition, you had to work out every day and dine with us in the chow hall. I emphasized discipline and bonding.

Our gang was less than half the size of rival squads, but when the fighting started 100 percent of our guys were ready to go, while 80 percent of their guys would abandon their group. So nobody wanted to go against us.

Our principles were put to a severe test when one of my guys told me a guy named Stoney was coming to our prison. A domestic-violence guy, a bad apple who beat up women, Stoney had beaten and killed the daughter of one of my members. As a matter of loyalty, we had no choice but to get him. If we didn't protect one of our own and avenge his daughter's death, then our whole way of doing things would be based on an empty promise.

As soon as Stoney entered the prison, he began attending the services of the Nation of Islam. New prisoners often did this to get protection. The Nation was powerful, not just in our prison, but in prisons nationwide. It provided the highest form of safety.

I called a meeting with Money Man, the head of the Nation of Islam. I explained that I had no choice but to take Stoney out. However, out of respect, I wanted to give him the chance to turn the guy over to me. Money Man took my request seriously, but replied, "Okay, you can have him—but one of your members killed one of my members' cousins. I need that guy in exchange."

Turning over one of my guys in a hostage exchange would violate our loyalty principle. So I came back with, "My guy is a member. The guy I want is your guest, not your member. That's not an exchange I'm willing to make."

We continued negotiating for three weeks with no progress. I had to make a choice: take Stoney out and risk war with the Nation of Islam or leave him alone and risk undermining my entire culture.

I chose the former. I talked to two of my most loyal members who were both doing life sentences and never getting out. I told them what needed to be done, and they did it without hesitation. Then we waited for the repercussions.

The repercussions never came. Our culture was so strong that not even the Nation of Islam wanted to go to war with us over a guest. Money Man ultimately respected our logic, backed by our strength.

My decision solidified our organization. But it also solidified an aspect of the culture that I did not intend. We were fucking savages.

Senghor had studied the culture, assimilated it, and meticulously improved it as he rose through the ranks. Once he reached the top of a gang, he was faced with a new set of choices—which prompted a profound realization. All those life-risking decisions he'd made, all those moments of serial integrity, had added up to a culture he didn't want.

Culture is weird like that. Because it's a consequence

of actions rather than beliefs, it almost never ends up exactly as you intend it. This is why it's not a "set it and forget it" endeavor. You must constantly examine and reshape your culture or it won't be your culture at all. Senghor was beginning to confront that classic problem.

At that point in my life, I was only focused on adherence to our internal code. I didn't think about forgiveness or any of that other stuff. I didn't think about how most of what we did caused somebody's family harm.

I first realized things could be different in 1995, when Louis Farrakhan and the Nation of Islam held the Million Man March. Leading up to the march, the prison authorities were in panic mode—they didn't know what might happen—and the guards started getting excessive with shakedowns. My guys reacted with all these half-cocked ideas.

The brothers come up to me and one of them, Hustle Man, says, "Me and Merch gonna stab some white guys for the Million Man March." In my head I'm like, This has got to be the dumbest shit ever. I'm like, This is not what my organization is about. Having self-love is not about hating other people. So I tell Hustle Man, "Since you feel so strongly about this, how about you go stab one of the white officers?" He like froze. I went on, "If you're not going to do that, then don't talk to me about stabbing these other guys who are being oppressed and locked down and going through the same shit as us." He just wanted an easy stabbing. He wasn't willing to do the hard shit. I knew that before I challenged him.

CHANGING THE CULTURE AND HIMSELF

Once Senghor realized the power of his influence, he began to make a concerted effort to shift the culture:

> One specific incident changed my internal compass. A football player got into a car accident in Detroit. A young lady crashed into him on a bridge. He jumped out of the car like he was going to attack her and she got scared and jumped off the bridge to get away and drowned. It became a big national story. When he was on his way to the joint, all these guys were saying, "We're going to stab this dude for what he did to the sister."
>
> And I was like, There are probably people's family members who think that about us. So I end up calling these guys out. And we have a tense-ass yard meeting.
>
> I'm like, "First of all, I don't even know this guy but ain't nobody gonna do shit to him." To explain why, I go around the group and say to the first guy, "What you in for?" And he goes, "Attempted murder." And I say: "Whoever you tried to kill, their family probably wants to fuck you up." I turn to the next guy and he goes, "Assault with intent to murder." I ask him how that guy's family would feel about that. As I continued around the group the guys gradually stepped outside of their bullshit and realized we had all made poor decisions and that we'd been fortunate that nobody had seen those decisions as stabbing-worthy. It was my way of getting at the implications of perpetuating violence and how two wrongs don't make a right.

The episode changed Senghor as much as it changed his squad. As a leader, you can float along in a morally ambiguous frame of mind until you face a clarifying choice. Then you either evolve or you wall yourself up in moral corruption.

Senghor used his incident as a catalyst:

I recognized my own hypocrisy when I chose to resolve conflicts by the rules of the yard as opposed to my own evolving principles. And I began to understand the different levels of how you shift an organization to be in line with your moral code.

It takes time, so I made it mandatory that we broke bread together, special meals of ramen noodles, summer sausage, cheese, or fresh ground beef or chicken. At our lunches we'd discuss the books that I'd sent out. That bonding and that sense of everybody feeling taken care of created a whole shift.

I wanted to change the culture so that when we went back to the community, we could help fix it for other kids. I could see that we all came from the same brokenness, the same fucked-upness. My analogy is this: imagine you're a developer and someone says, "Here's some land, and here's a million dollars. Could you build me a house on this land?" So you build this guy's dream home. And he moves in and then his family starts getting sick. Because what they didn't tell you is that the land is toxic and it was a fucking dump site.

The existing prison programs were surface-level shit. One was called "Stop Think Practice," or STP. The idea was that if you were about to get in trouble, and you stopped to think, then you'd behave better. Uh-huh. I took a psychotherapy class, but it didn't get into the real stuff. It didn't get into my mother nearly choking the life out of me over some bullshit. In one session, the instructor said, "You're probably never going to get out of here." How's that for psychotherapy? They were trying to build a dream home on a dump site. Nobody was digging into the dump site itself.

I utilized my position to set up daily classes like "Real Men, Real Talk," where we'd do deep dives on emotional intelligence. The classes were always packed, and we were able to dive into a lot of our bullshit. It got to a point where I would show up at a facility and the administration would be like, "Hey, would you help us organize some seminars on empathy and dealing with trauma?" So now I'm being entrusted by the same administration that was demonizing me.

Because I had maxed out what-the-fuck-you-can-become as a savage in prison, the guys knew I had nothing to gain from this—that I only wanted to make them better human beings. Now I see guys who are home and who benefited from that experience. They are thriving and living their lives the right way. That feels so much better.

Once he realized he had to make significant changes, Senghor knew that he had to align his team more tightly. He used one of the best techniques for changing a culture—constant contact. By requiring his team to eat together, work out together, and study together, he made them constantly aware of the cultural changes he was making. Nothing signals the importance of an issue like daily meetings about it.

WHO IS SHAKA SENGHOR NOW?

Senghor has been out of prison for ten years, is a best-selling author, and is a true leader in our society.

> I knew that there was a responsibility to talk to young people when I got out. When I looked back on my life I realized that I could have been anything. I could have been that doctor, I could have been that lawyer. How the fuck did I go from this kid with all this potential to this fucking prison-yard goon? I wanted my abilities to make my path, but the street culture ended up determining who I was.

Who is Shaka Senghor? Is he a ruthless criminal and prison gang leader, or a best-selling author, leader in prison reform, and contributor to a better society? Clearly he's capable of being both. That's the power of culture. If you want to change who you are, you have to change the culture you're in. Fortunately for the world he did. What he did is who he is.

5 SHAKA SENGHOR APPLIED

Big Poppa smash fools, bash fools
N*gg*s mad because I know that cash rules
—*Notorious B.I.G.*

Culture is an abstract set of principles that lives—or dies—by the concrete decisions the people in your organization make. As a leader, this gap between theory and practice poses huge challenges. How do you get an organization to behave when you're not around to supervise? How do you make sure the behaviors that you prescribe result in the culture that you want? How can you tell what's actually going on? How can you know if you've succeeded?

Two lessons for leaders jump out from Senghor's experience:

1. *Your own perspective on the culture is not that relevant.*
   Your view or your executive team's view of your culture is rarely what your employees experience. What Shaka

Senghor experienced on his first day out of quarantine transformed him. The relevant question is, What must employees do to survive and succeed in your organization? What behaviors get them included in, or excluded from, the power base? What gets them ahead?

2. *You must start from first principles.* Every ecosystem has a default culture. (In Silicon Valley, our baked-in cultural elements range from casual dress to employee owners to long hours.) Don't just blindly adopt it.

   • You may be adopting an organizing principle you don't understand. For example, Intel created a casual-dress standard to promote meritocracy. Its leaders believed the best idea should win, not the idea from the highest-ranking person in the fanciest suit. Many current Silicon Valley companies don't know that history, and adopt the casual dress without adopting the meritocracy that underpinned it.

   • And the predominant culture may not fit your business. Intel ran that way because the top engineers were as important in the decision-making process as the top executives. If you're in fast food, Intel's culture probably won't work for you.

Let's get into the details.

CULTURE CHANGES PEOPLE

Senghor walked into a culture that was designed to fix criminal behavior but that actually increases it. You have to ask why our prison system designed the culture that way. Do the people running it even know what the culture is or what it does?

If you're a leader, how do you know what *your* culture is? The question is harder than it sounds.

All leaders get surprised by feedback like "Our culture is really harsh" or "We're arrogant," but when they try to examine it directly to figure out what's going on, they fall prey to the *Heisenberg Uncertainty Principle of Management.* The act of trying to measure your culture changes the result. When you ask your managers, "What is our culture like?" they're likely to give you a managed answer that tells you what they think you want to hear and doesn't hint at what they think you absolutely do not want to hear. That's why they're called managers.

The best way to understand your culture is not through what managers tell you, but through how new employees behave. What behaviors do they perceive will help them fit in, survive, and succeed? That's your company's culture. Go around your managers to ask new employees these questions directly after their first week. And make sure you ask them for the bad stuff, the practices or assumptions that made them wary and uncomfortable. Ask them what's different than other places they've worked—not just what's better, but what's worse. And ask them for advice: "If you were me, how would you improve the culture based on your first week here? What would you try to enhance?"

Senghor told me the story of arriving at county jail, and then at prison, nearly thirty years after it happened, but he remembered it all like it was yesterday. Your first day, your first week in an organization is when you're observing each detail, figuring out where you stand. That's when your sense of the culture gets seared in—especially if someone gets stabbed in the neck.

That's when you diagnose the power structure: Who can get things done, and why? What did they do to get in that position? Can you replicate it? At the same time, how you behave on arrival—how other people see you—affects your standing and potential in the company and determines your personal brand.

First impressions of a culture are difficult to reverse. This is why new-employee orientation is better thought of as new-employee *cultural* orientation. Cultural orientation is your chance to make clear the culture you want and how you intend to get it. What behaviors will be rewarded? Which ones will be discouraged or severely punished? People's receptivity when they join, and the lasting impact of first impressions, is why the new-employee process is the most important one to get right. If your company's process for recruiting, interviewing, orienting, training, and integrating new employees is intentional and systematic, great. If any part of it is accidental, then so is your culture.

Many people believe that cultural elements are purely systematic, that employees only operate within a given corporate culture while they're in the office. The truth is that what people do at the office, where they spend most of their waking hours, becomes who they are. Office culture is highly infectious. If the CEO has an affair with an employee, there will be many affairs throughout the company. If profanity is rampant, most employees will take that home, too.

So trying to screen for "good people" or screen out "bad people" doesn't necessarily get you a high-integrity culture. A person may come in with high integrity but have to compromise it to succeed in your environment. Just as Africans in Saint-Domingue became the products of slave culture and then transformed into elite soldiers under Toussaint Louverture, people become the culture they live in and do what they have to do to survive and thrive.

LIVING THE CODE

Senghor's predecessors did not live up to their own code and it eventually cost them their positions. A leader must believe in his own code. Embedding cultural elements you don't subscribe to will eventually cause a cultural collapse.

As one example, I've never met a CEO who doesn't believe in the value of giving feedback. Everybody wants a transparent culture where people know where they stand. Yet I've met many CEOs who require managers to write performance reviews, but won't take the time to do it themselves. When I was CEO, I had a rule that everyone, including me, was held to: if you don't complete all your written performance reviews, nobody who works for you will receive their raises, bonuses, or stock-option increases. We always had 100 percent compliance on written feedback, because no manager wanted to be burned at the stake by her people. Cultural consistency on feedback was that important to me.

You could also argue that my rule was self-protective: over time, a hypocritical leader becomes vulnerable to being replaced by another, more walk-the-talk leader. Believing in your own principles is necessary, but not sufficient. You must also do as Senghor did and transfer those principles to your team in a way that sticks. Depending upon where the team is to begin with, this transfer may be a relatively minor effort or an immense undertaking. But it is critical, because it not only establishes the culture, but cements you as the leader.

If you are charismatic enough, you can sometimes get away with saying your culture is something it isn't. People will believe you, at least for a while. But you won't get the behaviors you need and you'll never become who you said you were.

CULTURE IS UNIVERSAL

You might think you can build a ruthlessly competitive culture that your employees use only to deal with outside forces but set aside when dealing with each other. You might think you can build an abusive, shame-you-for-your-failures culture that people participate in at work, but relinquish at quitting time. But that's not how it works. Cultural behaviors, once absorbed, get deployed everywhere.

Imagine you're a manager. Your company has the cultural value "We have each other's backs," meaning that you support one another when the chips are down. Now, imagine that one of your distribution partners is attempting to close a large deal and calls on one of your people for help, but your employee is busy and drops the ball—no show, no call, no help. The partner, furious at losing the deal through lack of support, calls you to vent. Do you have your employee's back or your partner's back? Is your allegiance to the culture or to the tribe?

If your allegiance is to the tribe, which is the more instinctive call, keep in mind that the idea behind supporting one another when the chips are down is to foster trust and loyalty throughout the company. It's nearly impossible for a company to be able to maintain one set of ethics with partners and an entirely different set in-house. If you support the employee, he will learn two lessons: 1) you have his back, and 2) dropping the ball is totally acceptable. The way you treat that partner will eventually be the way your employees treat each other.

As Senghor points out, culture travels.

WHEN THE CODE GETS WEAPONIZED

When a few members of Senghor's squad wanted to kill a couple of white prisoners, they were selfishly trying to manipulate the code. This move is common: Uber's CEO, Dara Khosrowshahi, refers to it as "weaponizing the culture." Senghor's guys were attempting to weaponize the cultural elements of "self-love and fighting oppression" to boost their own status. They could gain credibility as "killers" by picking an easy target. Senghor revealed their true motives by simply increasing the difficulty of the target—and the consequences of hitting it.

Stewart Butterfield, the founder and CEO of Slack, faced a similar situation when one of Slack's core cultural values, empathy, ended up with a lot of unintended consequences. (As the samurai realized, virtues are superior to values, but until that understanding becomes widespread, a lot of companies will continue to have values.) The empathy value was primarily aimed at customers, but it was also meant to improve communication internally by helping you understand your fellow workers better. If you are an engineer and you really understand the struggles of a product manager and the process she went through to get the customer data she's presenting, you'll take it more seriously.

But when employees got feedback from their managers that they needed to work more effectively with their peers or raise their overall game, a few weaponized the empathy value and fired back with "By giving me that feedback, you're not being empathetic!" Instead of using empathy to improve communication, these employees wanted to outlaw it because it hurt their feelings. Their pushback made some managers hesitate and begin to withhold feedback, fearing it might seem like unempathetic criticism.

Butterfield had to send a clear message about which behaviors were and were not part of the culture. So he began to shift the emphasis away from empathy and toward one of the core attributes he wanted to build into the culture: being collaborative. Then he defined what that value meant in practice. At Slack, "collaborative" means taking leadership from everywhere. Collaborative people know that their success is limited by uncollaborative people, so they are either going to help those people raise their game or they are going to get rid of them.

WHEN YOU HAVE TO CHANGE YOURSELF TO CHANGE YOUR CULTURE

Cultures tend to reflect the values of the leaders. Ultimately, Senghor had to change himself to get the culture that he wanted. Business leaders face the same challenges, but often assume that they are "good people" and ignore their own shortcomings. This produces dangerous cultural consequences.

I had many of these moments when I was the CEO of LoudCloud, and each of them felt like they could go either way. Once, after a quarter that was strong on revenue but low on bookings—an accounting term for guaranteed contracts that will eventually become revenue—some of my employees devised an elaborate way to make an unguaranteed contract sound like a booking. Basically, the team suggested that we toss actual bookings and unguaranteed contracts into the same bucket. I really did not want to miss our bookings number, and technically the proposal was not a lie or illegal, so could I get away with it? I was leaning toward trying to. That is, I was willing to be deceptive as long as I could claim that we had followed the letter of the law—and therefore been truthful.

Then Jordan Breslow, my general counsel, came by and said, "Ben, this whole discussion is making me very uncomfortable." I said, "Jordan, why? We're not saying anything that's not true, and if we miss the bookings number, that might lead to a blizzard of bad press followed by customers not trusting us and us missing another quarter and being forced to do a layoff." He said, "Yes, but we are proposing to tell the truth in such a way that what people hear is not true." I thought: Oh no, he's right.

I then made a rule that we would only report numbers related to revenue that were defined by standard accounting law and that had been audited by an outside firm. I had to change in order for us to change our culture from *telling the truth* to *making sure people heard the truth.* This shift derived from our original cultural goal of *trust.* Trust, as I discussed in the Louverture chapter, is the foundation of communication. Simply saying something you feel more or less comfortable terming "the truth" doesn't build trust. What builds trust is the bona fide truth being heard.

But I genuinely might have gone the other way if Breslow hadn't stopped me. Culture can feel abstract and secondary when you pit it against a concrete result that's right in front of you. Culture is a strategic investment in the company doing things the right way when you are not looking.

CHANGE CULTURE THROUGH CONSTANT CONTACT

When Senghor decided to dramatically redirect the Melanics, he did it through urgent emphasis in daily meetings. This is one of the best ways to change culture in a company.

I recently recommended to Lea Endres, CEO of Nation-Builder, which builds software for community leaders, that she follow Senghor's lead. NationBuilder was operating close to the red and Endres was frustrated because, despite her reminding everyone that cash collection was a priority, she couldn't get her team to care enough about it. Our conversation went like this:

LEA: I'm really worried about cash collections. We use this outsourced finance firm and they don't care. We have a low cash balance and we got surprised last month. A couple more surprises and we're in deep trouble.

BEN: Is there a team on it? How much do you need to collect this month?

LEA: Yes. And $1.1 million at least.

BEN: If you have a crisis situation and you need the team to execute, meet with them every day and even twice a day if necessary. That will show them this is a top priority. At the beginning of each meeting you say, "Where's my money?" They will start making excuses like "Boo Boo was supposed to call me and didn't," or "The system didn't tell me the right thing." Those excuses are the key, because that's the knowledge you're missing. Once you know that the excuse is that "Fred didn't answer my email," you can tell Fred to answer the damned email and also tell the person making the excuse that you expect way more persistence. The meetings will start out running long, but two weeks later they'll be short, because when you say, "Where's my money?" they are going to want to say, "Right here, Lea!"

Two weeks later:

LEA: You wouldn't believe some of the excuses. One was that we have an auto email that is one sentence long that tells customers they are late—but it doesn't tell them what to do! I'm like, "Well, then, let's fix the damned email!" We're making progress and they know I want my money.

End of quarter:

LEA: We collected $1.6 million in September! And the team loves hearing me say "Where's my money?!?!"

To change a culture, you can't just give lip service to what you want. Your people must *feel* the urgency of it.

6 GENGHIS KHAN, MASTER OF INCLUSION

Inter century anthems based off inner city tantrums
Based off the way we was branded
Face it, Jerome get more time than Brandon
And at the airport they check all through my bag and
Tell me that it's random.
—*Kanye West, "Gorgeous"*

Genghis Khan was the most effective military leader in history. He conquered more than twice as much land as anyone else, and he did it in a series of astonishing campaigns. He subdued some twelve million square miles—an area roughly the size of Africa, stretching from the Persian Gulf to the Arctic Ocean—with an army of just one hundred thousand men.

Most companies today struggle with how to create an inclusive culture, but Genghis Khan mastered this difficult art nearly a thousand years ago. He subsumed peoples from China and Persia and Europe, practitioners of Islam,

Buddhism, Christianity, and even cannibalism, within one contiguous domain. He built his realm on such firm foundations that after his death it continued growing for 150 years.

How could a fearful boy named Temujin, who shrank from dogs and cried at the slightest provocation, who grew up an outcast in a tiny nomadic tribe in the middle of nowhere, achieve such feats? What cultural innovations enabled this success?

Temujin was born in 1162 in one of the harshest, most arid regions of the world, near the modern-day border of Mongolia and Siberia. According to *The Secret History of the Mongols*, a court history, he emerged from the womb clutching a large clot of blood, an augury that he would be a conqueror. Both the bloodshed and the augury would prove prophetic.

Temujin was raised in a small tribe of Tayichiud, one of the two leading clans among the thirteen that made up the Mongols. His father, Yesugei, a middle-rank clan leader, had kidnapped his mother, Hoelun, to make her his second wife. Kidnapping a prospective wife was a standard move at the time; Hoelun, then fifteen, was already married. The new couple named their first boy Temujin, after a warrior whom Yesugei had captured and executed named Temujin Uge. Not exactly *Leave it to Beaver*, but a fitting origin for the man who would become The Great Khan.

We don't know how Temujin looked as a boy, but in *Genghis Khan: His Conquests, His Empire, His Legacy*, Frank McLynn writes that as an adult he was formidable:

"robustly healthy, tall, broad-browed, with a long beard and eyes like a cat," all of which "made him appear calm, ruthless, calculating and self-controlled." His worldview, Temujin himself would later declare, was piratical:

It is delightful and felicitous for a man to subdue rebels and conquer and extirpate his enemies, to take all they possess, to cause their servants to cry out, to make tears run down their faces and noses, to ride their pleasant-paced geldings, to make the bellies and navels of their wives his bed and bedding, to use the bodies of his women as a nightshirt.

That was the Mongol way. When Temujin was eight or nine, his father took him along as he rode out to seek a wife for the boy. During their search among nearby clans, they stayed with a family who had a daughter named Borte. The children liked each other and the fathers agreed to betroth them. Temujin would remain with Borte's family as a herder while his father raised the bride price, and then they would marry.

Three years later, Yesugei ate a meal with the Tatars, the tribe of Temujin Uge, the warrior he had killed. Apparently he failed to sufficiently hide his identity, and they poisoned him. As he was dying, Yesugei sent for Temujin, who was forced to leave Borte and her family and return home—to a family that now consisted of two widows and seven small children.

Unwilling to support so many hungry mouths, the Tayichiud abandoned the family and stole their animals, essentially condemning them to death on the harsh steppe. Hoelun kept her family going through sheer will: they wore the skins of the dogs and mice that they ate to keep from starving.

Temujin chafed under the bullying of his older half brother Begter, now the family's eldest male. Not only did Begter eat the fish that Temujin had caught, but he seemed eager to begin sleeping with his widowed stepmother, Hoelun, as was traditional. Temujin's solution to the problem was extremely direct: he and his younger brother Khasar took their bows and shot Begter full of arrows. Kids, let that be a lesson to you: don't pick on your younger brother, as he may turn out to be Genghis Khan.

Hoelun was furious. How could the boys hope to build alliances and avenge themselves on their tribe if they couldn't even refrain from murdering their half brother? "You are like wolves," she said, "like mad dogs that tear their own flesh."

To punish this killing, the Tayichiud captured Temujin and made him a slave, working him hard. Temujin soon escaped and was taken in by a poor family that hid him under fleeces when his captors came in search of him. This kindness from strangers, contrasted with his treatment by his rich kin the Tayichiud, made a strong impression. In *Genghis Kahn and the Making of the Modern World,* Jack Weatherford observes that the experience gave Temujin "the conviction that some people, even those outside his clan, could indeed be trusted as if they were family. In later life, he would judge others primarily by their actions toward him and not according to their kinship bonds, a revolutionary concept in steppe society." As we shall see, judging others primarily by their actions is also a revolutionary concept in many of today's corporate cultures.

In 1178, Temujin turned sixteen. Though he had not seen his intended wife, Borte, since his father died, he felt confident enough to seek her out again. He was pleased to discover that she had waited for him. By custom a new bride brought a gift for the groom's parents. Borte brought a coat of black sable, the most prized fur on the steppe. Temujin shrewdly gave the coat to a man named Ong Khan, one of his father's old allies, expecting that he'd need allies of his own.

He needed them almost immediately. After eighteen years of biding its time, Hoelun's original tribe, the Merkid, took its vengeance for her abduction, falling on Temujin's camp with some three hundred men. Temujin and his brothers were able to ride away, but Borte was captured and given to an older Merkid man as his wife.

Temujin's clan was no match for the powerful Merkids, and most men in his position would have simply looked around for a new wife to kidnap. But though Mongol men were reserved, Temujin openly lamented that the Merkids had cut open his chest and broken his heart. Choosing to fight, he went to Ong Khan, who agreed to help. Ong Khan sent Temujin to get additional aid from a rising young Mongol, Jamuka of the Jadaran clan. Jamuka and Temujin were already blood brothers—they had played knucklebones together as children—so Jamuka signed on, too. With these powerful friends, Temujin was ready for battle.

One night Temujin's posse fell upon the Merkids, routing them. Temujin began searching the tents for Borte. She had been loaded into a cart and sent away from the battle for safety. *The Secret History* describes how, amid the sounds of conflict, Borte recognized a voice crying her name. Jumping from the cart, she raced through the darkness toward the voice. Temujin was so distraught that when she ran up and snatched the reins of his horse, he almost attacked her. Then he recognized her, and they "threw themselves upon each other." Though Borte was pregnant by her Merkid husband, Temujin adopted the child as his own. Blood lineage truly meant little to him.

Despite his blood brother Jamuka's help in rescuing Borte, Temujin began to clash with him. Once again, caste played a significant part in the conflict. In Mongol kinship hierarchy, each lineage was known as a bone. The closest lineages to the leader were considered superior and known as white bones. More distant lineages were black bones. As long as Temujin was part of Jamuka's band, he was black-boned kin to a white bone. Only if he established his own band would Temujin be considered white-boned.

Having murdered his own brother rather than submit to him, Temujin was not going to bow to Jamuka. In 1183, their tribes split. It took twenty years of bitter fighting—interrupted by periodic truces and oaths of fealty—for Temujin to finally conquer Jamuka, sweep up the other independent tribes, and become the de facto leader of all the Mongols.

In 1206, the Mongol nobles gathered and asked Temujin to become their supreme leader. He accepted under the condition that every Mongol obey him without question, go wherever on earth he directed, and put to death whomever he chose. Now that he was in charge of thirty-one tribes and some two million Mongols, Temujin took the name Genghis Khan, meaning "fierce" or "tough" ruler.

The Mongols had always been divided against themselves, with tribes and clans and bands ceaselessly teaming up to battle a common enemy and then falling out to fight each other. Every noble on the steppe, even the lowliest brigand, believed he should rule over all. Genghis realized that these warlords needed a common goal, and that it should be predicated not on the aristocrats' dream of primacy, but rather on his soldiers' primal desires. Genghis grasped that he could motivate them with "huge and exponential amounts of booty," as McLynn puts it. This, in fact, would be their only form of payment.

> The aim was to ensure loyalty to the khan, not to tribe or clan, and this loyalty could be secured if the rewards were big enough. . . . To keep his superstate in being, Genghis needed constant influxes of wealth, and that meant permanent conquest and war; too long a period of peace would encourage the powerful and frustrated custodians of his commonwealth to turn in on, and eventually against, themselves.

After putting all the Mongol tribes under his yoke, Genghis attacked and subdued northern China. Then he turned west and knifed through Khwarezmia, the Persian Empire. And finally, before he died in 1227—most likely from the effects of a fall from his horse—he brought Russia under his thumb.

Genghis's campaigns were ruthless. His generals routinely told opposing forces they would spare them if they surrendered, then, when they did, butchered them all. After conquering the city of Gurganj, his army made the women strip naked and fight each other before they slaughtered them. In many cities Genghis wiped out not only the people, but even the dogs, cats, and rats. He spared only the artisans, who were sent back to Mongolia. In the Arab world to which he laid waste, he became known as "the Accursed One."

But he also, contrarily, displayed a new kind of acceptance and inclusiveness.

HOW CULTURE AFFECTED MILITARY STRATEGY

Genghis Khan's sweeping meritocracy made his army fundamentally different from—and more powerful than—any that came before it.

In most armies, the leaders were on horseback while everyone else was slow-moving infantry; Genghis's army consisted entirely of cavalry, so they were all equals and they all moved fast. Most armies had large units dedicated to providing supplies; in Genghis's army, each man carried what he needed: clothes for all weathers, flints for making fires, canteens for water and milk, files to sharpen arrowheads, a lasso for rounding up animals or prisoners, sewing needles for mending clothes, a knife and a hatchet for cutting, and a skin bag for packing it all. They all milked their animals and fed themselves from hunting and looting.

Traditional armies, hierarchical and class based, moved in long columns that marched in one direction trailed by large supply units. The Mongols were organized in concentric circles. Each squad of ten men was part of a brigade of one thousand, a new "tribe" Genghis created to replace the Mongols' hereditary ones. These brigades, in turn, were part of a battalion of ten thousand men. At the pinnacle of the army's power, ten of these ten-thousand-man battalions encircled Genghis Khan, who rode in the middle.

This structure enabled the Mongols to outmaneuver, surround, and destroy their enemies. Mongol forces routinely defeated armies five times their size. And they often confounded conventional wisdom by attacking on two fronts at once, a tactic that forestalled neighboring princes from coming to each other's aid, lest the next attack suddenly land on their own city. Genghis's campaigns were marked by rapid advances—his cavalry could move sixty-five miles a day, and Mongolian ponies were as nimble as dogs—by clouds of arrows, alternate attacks from light and heavy cavalry, feigned retreats and frequent ambushes, and an unsporting reluctance to engage in hand-to-hand combat. They were guerrilla warriors who happened to have an army. The Jin people of China were only the first to be astonished by the Mongols' mercurial strikes: "They come as though the sky were falling, and they disappear like a flash of lightning."

As his armies surged forward, Genghis made sure that the best practices among the newly conquered were transmitted throughout his domain. In this way, the entire empire rose as one. Weatherford writes:

> Whether in their policy of religious tolerance, devising a universal alphabet, maintaining relay stations, playing games, or printing almanacs, money, or astronomy charts, the rulers of the Mongol Empire displayed a persistent universalism. Because they had no system of their own to impose upon their subjects, they were willing to adopt and combine systems from everywhere. Without deep cultural preferences in these areas, the Mongols implemented pragmatic rather than ideological solutions. They searched for what worked best; and when they found it, they spread it to other countries.

Genghis created a remarkably stable culture by founding it on three principles: meritocracy, loyalty, and inclusion.

MERITOCRACY

After uniting the Mongols in 1189, Temujin made his first organizational innovation. In most steppe tribes, the khan's court was an aristocracy consisting of his relatives. Weatherford writes:

Temujin, however, assigned some dozen responsibilities to various followers according to the ability and loyalty of the individual without regard to kinship. He gave the highest positions as his personal assistants to his first two followers, Boorchu and Jelme, who had shown persistent loyalty to him for more than a decade.

Mongol women were already treated unusually well for the time, but Genghis went on to abolish inherited aristocratic titles and eliminate the caste hierarchy; all men were equal. Shepherds and camel boys could now become generals. Temujin called all his subjects "the People of the Felt Walls"—the material used for the walls of their *gers*, or yurts. This symbolized that they were a single clan.

To solidify this new meritocracy, he made it a capital offense for his family members to become a khan, or leader, without being elected to the post. He introduced the concept of the rule of law; might alone no longer made right. At a time when rulers considered themselves above the law, Genghis Khan insisted that leaders be as accountable as the lowest herder.

There was just one exception to this principle: Genghis himself. At his worst he behaved like any other despot. And he further weakened the meritocracy by favoring his own children with huge land grants after they complained that they'd been bypassed by commoners. McLynn writes, "To the question 'Was Mongol society under Genghis Khan a rule-governed system or a tyranny?' the answer can only be: both."

Yet for a leader of his time, Genghis was remarkably down-to-earth; he walked the talk. While he expected obeisance, he never portrayed himself as godlike—indeed, he never allowed anyone to paint his portrait, sculpt his image, or engrave his name or likeness on a coin. In a letter to a Taoist monk, Genghis spoke of himself as just another soldier, saying, "I have not myself distinguished qualities," and adding, "I continue to wear the same clothing and eat the same food as the cowherds and horse-herders. We make the same sacrifices, and we share the riches."

By converting his army from a genetic hierarchy to a true meritocracy, Genghis Khan rid himself of the idlers and mediocrities who rule in an aristocracy, raised the army's talent level considerably, and inspired ambitious soldiers to dream that if they proved courageous and intelligent, they, too, could lead.

LOYALTY

Genghis Khan defined loyalty quite differently from his contemporaries. Typically, leaders asked warriors to die for them, but Genghis viewed loyalty as a bilateral relationship that gave him significant responsibilities. When two horse wranglers warned of a plot against him, he made them generals. After his troops captured one of Jamuka's archers, who'd nearly killed Temujin with a long shot, the archer explained to Temujin that it was nothing personal; he'd had to follow his leader's orders. The archer expected to be put to death, but Temujin made him an officer, and he went on to become a great general.

Genghis's purpose in battle was to preserve Mongol life. He preferred to conquer through intimidation that led to surrender, so towns that capitulated immediately were often afforded leniency while those that resisted had their citizens marched in front of his army as human shields. (As I noted earlier, Genghis was moody and his generals could be impulsive, so his forces didn't always adhere to this principle.) When one of his soldiers was killed, Genghis ordered that his share of the loot be distributed to his widow and children.

Unique among conquerors, Genghis never punished any of his generals, which explains why, across six decades, none of them deserted or betrayed him. Using a technique later employed by Shaka Senghor, Genghis demanded that his army's ethics apply to outsiders as well. When he declared that you must never betray your khan, he intended it as a global rule. After he defeated Jamuka at last, in 1205, some of Jamuka's men turned their leader over to him, hoping to gain Genghis's favor. Rather than rewarding these turncoats, he executed them—just as Jamuka had warned them he would. And then he executed Jamuka.

By elevating loyalty to a higher principle, Genghis created a massive military advantage. Precisely because he wasn't asking his troops to die for him, they eagerly would. The Mongols said about the Great Khan that "If he sends me into fire or water I go. I go for him."

INCLUSION

Genghis instituted a radical change in the protocols of warfare. Rather than treating conquered aristocratic leaders with special care and enslaving the rank and file, he executed the aristocrats (so they couldn't later rise against him) and incorporated the soldiers into his army. In this way he not only swelled his ranks, but also established himself as an equal-opportunity employer, the guy whose team you wanted to be on.

After he defeated the Jurkin clan in 1196, he had his mother, Hoelun, adopt a Jurkin boy and raise him as a son. This made clear that the conquered would share in future conquests as though they were part of the original tribe. To symbolize the new equality, Genghis threw a feast for the defeated Mongols and their new relatives. He also encouraged intermarriage to further integrate the tribes.

Anyone could have added enemy soldiers into his army—everyone from the Romans on had—but Genghis's stroke of brilliance was treating those soldiers so well that they became more loyal to him than to their original leaders.

This approach was crystallized in 1203, when he was being pursued by Ong Khan, his former mentor. Temujin took refuge in the swamp, near northern China, and there he and nineteen of his commanders drank water from the Baljuna River and swore an oath. The commanders swore lifelong allegiance to Genghis, who swore lifelong loyalty to them. As Weatherford writes:

The nineteen men with Temujin Khan came from nine different tribes; probably only Temujin and his brother Khasar were actually from the Mongol clans. The others included Merkid, Khitan, and Kereyid. Whereas Temujin was a devout shamanist who worshiped the Eternal Blue Sky and the God Mountain of Burkhan Khaldun, the nineteen included several Christians, three Muslims, and several Buddhists. They were united only in their devotion to Temujin and their oath to him and each other. The oaths sworn at Baljuna created a type of brotherhood, and in transcending kinship, ethnicity, and religion, it came close to being a type of modern civic citizenship based upon personal choice and commitment.

When the highly civilized Uighur people surrendered without a fight in 1209, Genghis deployed many of their officials throughout his realm as judges, generals, scribes, secret agents, and tax collectors. McLynn notes that this was another pivotal moment:

Since their high skills, talents, and culture had been placed at the service of the Mongols, and their script accepted as the first official language of the governing class, they helped to give the empire ideological and spiritual legitimacy; it could no longer be said that this was just a congeries of cruel, bloodthirsty savages.

As Genghis extended his reach, he became more selective about who he incorporated into his army, focusing on scholars and engineers as well as doctors, who rode with each of his thousand-man brigades. After having great success using Chinese scholars to administer the empire, every time he captured a city he would have its scholars brought in for interrogation—essentially interviewing them for open job postings. By incorporating foreign engineers, he captured the knowledge needed to build the most technically advanced fighting force ever assembled; in this way he adopted such weapons as the trebuchet and the catapult.

After Genghis's death in 1227, the Mongols who inherited his empire continued his cross-cultural approach with spectacular results. Their engineers combined elements from China (gunpowder) and the Islamic world (flamethrowers) inside a European innovation (casting metal bells), to create a new and awesome weapon: the cannon.

Genghis codified many aspects of inclusiveness into law. He outlawed kidnapping women and made it illegal to sell them into marriage (even as his warriors continued to rape and take concubines from among the defeated). He declared all children to be legitimate, thereby eliminating the concept of illegitimate or lesser people. And he introduced, perhaps for the first time anywhere, total religious freedom. While conquered peoples had to swear allegiance to Genghis and had to obey the Mongols' common law—and while he executed clerics and imams who preached against him—they could otherwise believe what they liked and follow their own laws. He was a pragmatist, not a zealot.

There were inevitable problems with cultural hybridization. After being exposed for the first time to alcoholic beverages stronger than their fermented mares' milk, many Mongols, including Genghis and much of his immediate family, became drunkards. And Genghis's decentralization of power would lead to succession problems after his death, when he allowed his sons and their successors to essentially divide his land into separate khanates, or "ulus." McLynn writes:

> From an administrative point of view, Genghis took the correct decision, as his empire was too vast and unwieldy for a strongly centralised ruler to control; but humanly and politically it was a very great mistake and, not surprisingly, it was precisely along the fault lines of the ulus settlement that the empire would eventually break up—and the problem was compounded by the Mongols' integration with other cultures.

Still, it was an extraordinary empire while it lasted, and it was built on cultural innovation. Because he had grown up as an outcast, Genghis Khan saw what blinded other leaders in his day and indeed most leaders even today. Where they perceived only differences, only threats they would be prudent to suppress, Genghis Khan saw only talent he could use.

7 INCLUSION IN THE MODERN WORLD

I wear every single chain, even when I'm in the house
'Cause we started from the bottom, now we're here.
—*Drake*

Times have changed since Genghis Khan mastered inclusion. Is it still a cultural tool that will enable you to conquer the known world? We explore the potential power—as well as some of the pitfalls—of trying to create an inclusive culture.

FROM CABRINI-GREEN TO CEO

The self-help guru Tony Robbins says the quality of your life is a function of the quality of questions you ask yourself. If you ask, "Why am I so fat?" your brain will say, "Because I am stupid and have no willpower." Robbins's point is that if you ask a bad question you will get a bad answer and you will live a bad life. But if you ask, "How can I use my vast resources to get into the best shape of my life?" your brain will say, "I will eat the highest-quality healthy food, work out like a professional athlete, and live to be one hundred and twenty."

As a society, we often ask, "Why do we have so few African-American CEOs of Fortune 500 companies?" And we get answers like "Racism, Jim Crow, slavery, and structural inequality." Perhaps we should be asking, "How in the world did a black kid from the notorious Chicago housing project Cabrini-Green Gardens become the only African-American CEO of McDonald's?" If we want to figure out why inclusion hasn't worked, we ask the former. As we want to figure out how to make inclusion work, we should ask the latter.

Genghis Khan overcame being a black bone and an outcast to conquer much of the world and then remake it in a more egalitarian way. His tactics included killing his half brother Begter and his blood brother Jamuka as well as countless others. That doesn't work so well in today's world. Don Thompson rose through a very different approach: he embraced inclusion from the bottom up, forging alliances rather than forcing people to accept them. But once he had power he employed egalitarian techniques remarkably similar to Genghis's. They both saw people not through the prism of their rank or color but for who they were and who they could become, if given the opportunity.

At six feet four and 265 pounds, Thompson is physically intimidating. Yet he is so affable and genuine that if you don't like Don Thompson, you don't like yourself. His philosophy about people and race reflects his disarming demeanor. As he told me:

> There are two ways to approach being the only black guy in the meeting. You can think, "Everyone is looking at me"—and start sliding down the slippery slope: "They don't like me, they don't like black people . . ." Or you can think, as I do, "Everyone is looking at me and they have no idea of the experience that is about to hit them in the face called Don Thompson. I'm going to go and talk to them and they will learn about me and I will learn about them and we might even strike up a wonderful friendship that leads to a long-lasting business relationship."
>
> Unfortunately, a lot of our folks have been brainwashed to approach life in the first way. A meeting is a game. I'm trying to figure you out and you're trying to figure me out. Can we be partners, can we be assets to each other, or are we going to be enemies? If you start the game thinking everyone in the room is your enemy, you've already lost. You must reset your framework to thinking that you're bringing the new stuff, the good stuff, the stuff they don't have.

Thompson was raised by his grandmother, Rosa, in what he affectionately refers to as the Neighborhood, rather than the 'hood. That subtle tweak in terminology pervades Thompson's outlook—where others see bleakness, he sees opportunity. Cabrini-Green was almost entirely African-American. Its only white residents were a cop, a fireman, and an insurance salesman. The salesman sold life insurance policies just large enough to cover the cost of a funeral.

When Thompson was ten they moved to Indianapolis. His neighborhood was still African-American, but now his school was mostly white. Rosa taught Thompson how to negotiate these different worlds: she was a manager at Ayr-Way, a midmarket retail chain later acquired by Target. Most of her employees were white, but she treated everyone the same, and they all visited the house. Thompson learned from her that people can be good or bad, but you had to look at them individually to see who was what.

When Thompson entered Purdue University, in 1979, he got a shock. He recalls:

My first night on campus, I am so excited to be at college and a convertible pulls up with three white guys in it and they shout, "Nigger!"

I was stunned, but it was game on. Because there is no way in this world that you are going to deter me from what I am here for. I've seen you before. I may not have seen you specifically, but I've seen people just like you. But I've also seen black folks who tried to hold me around the neck and strangle me to death. Ain't nothin' new to me. Stop the car if you want to, all three of you against me. We can do that. Or keep driving and yell what you want to, because that ain't gonna change nothing.

Nonetheless, he remains grateful for his time at Purdue—and now serves on the university's board of trustees.

Regardless of where you are from, if you come out of here with this engineering degree, you will have earned it. And that felt equal.

After graduating in 1984, Thompson took an engineering job at Northrop in the Defense Systems Division. Things started poorly there, too:

Bro, I got a desk. My own desk! I go in the first day and what's taped on the middle of it? A white cross. I scraped it off, balled it up, and put it in the garbage can. And then I put my stuff in my desk. Remembering the words of my grandmother, I ignored the incident and went on to establish some really great relationships.

Thompson spent the next six years at Northrop and moved into management. When the defense sector softened in the late 1980s, he got a call from a recruiter asking him if he wanted to come work at McDonald's. He naturally assumed it was McDonnell Douglas, the defense contractor:

When I found out it was McDonald's hamburgers, my response was "No, thank you." I worked too hard to become an electrical engineer, and my grandmother invested too much in me for me to end up flipping hamburgers. They had a McDonald's guy call me who had been an engineer at Bell Labs. He said, "What do you have to lose by coming in to talk?" It was a lesson for me. Now I say, "Don't turn down anything except your collar."

Thompson began in the engineering group, helping McDonald's make the most delicious french fries in the world by optimizing a process known as "the fry curve." The fry curve is the temperature curve a french fry travels during its cooking cycle. Optimizing the curve is tricky, because the fries enter the hot oil at various temperatures, sometimes lukewarm and sometimes straight from the freezer. Thompson and his team inserted a computer chip into the fryer and programmed it to ensure that McDonald's fries traveled the optimal curve every time. By excelling at this and other challenges, he became the top engineer in the department. And that nearly led to his leaving the company:

McDonald's gave the President's Award every year to the top one percent of performers. I had a great year and everyone in the department kept saying, "Don, there is no way you will not win the President's Award for engineering." The day of the awards, I was dressed to a T and cleaner than the board of health. I was so excited. And then they announced that there were no winners in the engineering department. The year before we had had two.

So I went to the pity party. I told myself, "They didn't want a black person to win. They are not ready for me. I'm going to quit." The head of the department came up and said, "You're probably wondering why you didn't win." I said, "As a matter of fact I am." He said, "Because I didn't put your name in. We had two winners last year." So now I am not only ready to attend the pity party, I am ready to host it.

I call the people I know and tell them I am going to leave. And one of them says, "Before you decide, I want you to talk to Raymond Mines. Just do me a favor and meet him."

Raymond Mines, who ran a McDonald's region that covered eight states, from Washington to Michigan, was one of the company's top two African-American leaders. He was a really rough guy from the neighborhoods in Ohio. When I met with this dude, he said, "Why are you leaving?" I said, "Obviously McDonald's is not ready for me. They are not ready for the kind of impact I can make." He said, "So you're leaving because you didn't get the award." He cut right to the chase. Then he said, "The quality management group wants you. They are willing to promote you, so why don't you go work for them?" And he added, "And maybe one day you can come work for me."

I thought, That has to be the most arrogant comment I have ever heard. Still, what Raymond said kept bothering me. I was expecting sympathy and all I got from him was strength. It kind of shocked me out of my own b.s. So I took the job.

Thompson was now one of four people working on quality management at McDonald's. The other three had the plum jobs of writing speeches for the top execs; he drew the short straw of carrying the flip charts to meetings around the globe. But this task enabled him to learn, and then to master, the complex operations of the world's largest restaurant business. He met nearly every significant group in the company and pieced together the process flows, the subcultures of the different operating units and the relationships between them, the details of the business model—the hidden magic that made the hamburger factory hum.

> *I got the view from the bottom. We would have objectives to get people to smile more or work harder, but when I got to a restaurant I would find out that someone was working at McDonald's for eight hours and then going to their other job for eight hours. To be effective at that level, you really had to understand what the employees were going through.*

A year in, when Thompson passed Raymond Mines in the hall, Mines cried, "It's time to pay the piper!" He had created a new position in his region for Thompson: Director of Strategic Planning. Thompson shadowed Mines as he inspected the regions, resolved local issues, and set the plans for each quarter and year. Mines had an unusual management style:

> *I would get a call on a Thursday and Raymond would say, "Meet me at the airport on Monday." I would ask, "Where are we going? How long are we going to be*

there?" and he'd say, "Never mind where we're going, pack for three days."

I'd show up at the airport and we'd fly to a region that might be having a dispute with its restaurants and he'd say, "Don, you resolve it." Now, in the region we covered all the restaurant managers were white, and at first they were like, "Don, get the fuck out of here." But I worked it and got things resolved and learned everything I had not learned in the previous job. This job gave me the view from the top.

I was tasked with helping the regional managers improve their business. Well, if I walked in saying that, I'd instantly become the enemy. With Raymond's coaching, I developed a much more effective approach. I would say, "Look, I am here to help in any way I can. I'm not coming in to tell you what to do. What I can do is help you understand your performance relative to other regions and help you hit your plan." That approach changed the whole dynamic. If you are the one guy wanting to help, then the regional managers would embrace you. Those white guys taught me all the details of how to be a regional manager, which directly led to my ascent to CEO.

Recognizing that it was the jobs that he took after he decided to quit that prepared him most to be CEO, Thompson drew two lessons on how to succeed as a minority:

1. Don't attend pity parties. *And definitely don't host them.*

2. Don't turn down anything except your collar. *Oppor-tunities can come from anywhere. You ask an electrical engineer to design the thermal system on the french fryer. Then you ask me to carry flip charts to facilitate strategic planning. I had many reasons to refuse all the opportunities that led to me becoming CEO.*

His own bumpy rise—where he'd had to make his own way, but also be open to grabbing a helping hand at a crucial juncture—informed his philosophy and his approach to inclusion and diversity as McDonald's CEO:

The company had a women's network, an African-American network, a Latino network, and a gay and lesbian network. One day I see a lot of the white guys together, and they said, "Don, we have a question. Who's thinking about us?" I said, "What do you mean?" They said, "You got networks for blacks, Latinos, and gays—but who's thinking about us? What network do we have?"

A lot of people would have replied, "Are you fucking kidding me?" But Thompson has the rare gift of being able to hear a comment that could easily sound insensitive or self-involved and to perceive the underlying anxiety. He hears the context and the intent that most cannot.

So I said, "You know what? We need a white male network." They said, "Stop messing with us." I said, "I'm serious. Are we about true diversity and inclusion or are we about black folks' rights, Latino rights, and all that?" The point was, Do we want to see people for who they are and get the best of everyone or do we just want to advocate for certain groups over others? So we created the first white male network. They didn't want to call it that, of course, so we called it the Inclusion Network.

I asked Thompson to elaborate on his unusual approach.

The other networks thought I had lost my mind. They said, "They don't need a network, they're the majority." I said, "Right now, today, they are the majority. I get it. But you have to ask yourself, What do you really stand for? You claim to stand for diversity. Well, that means every idea in this room merits some inclusion. And if that's the case then we must include white men, too. Either you're inclusive or you're not."

After creating the Inclusion Network, Thompson took all the network leaders on a retreat. On that retreat, he tried to pass on a lesson that Genghis Khan had learned and exploited nearly a thousand years earlier. *Don't see me as a bastard or a black bone. See me as a first-class citizen and I will help you conquer the world.*

The retreat started with each group talking about its concerns about all of the others. After hours of listening to these identical complaints, everyone concluded that

*their concerns were totally unfounded, because every-
one there wanted the same damned thing. They all
wanted to be seen and heard and included in the conversation. Most of all, they wanted to be valued. That's
what inclusion needs to be about. Do you see a black
man, or do you see Don?*

If the key to effective inclusion is seeing people for
who they are, then how do we make sure that we really
see them?

LOYALTY AND MERITOCRACY TODAY

Many modern corporations employ a subtle caste system. Your social strata is determined not by being white-
boned or black-boned, but by whether you're blue-collar
or white-collar, or whether you went to Stanford or Michigan State. In Silicon Valley, it is often determined by
whether or not you can code.

When Maggie Wilderotter, who'd been head of global
strategy at Microsoft, took over Frontier Communications in 2004, she was confronted by one of the starkest
class systems in modern business.

Frontier, a Baby Bell spun off from the breakup of AT&T,
made most of its money providing local and long-distance
phone service. It had two classes of employees: white-collar
and blue-collar. The white-collar personnel were mostly
in the company's headquarters in Norwalk, Connecticut;
the blue-collar workers were spread throughout Frontier's

15,000 markets in rural and suburban America. Because the latter dealt with the company's customers, they were the true face of Frontier. Yet the executives treated them like peasants, and almost never flew out to the regions to understand what they were actually doing day-to-day. Meanwhile, the executives had a corporate doctor, a corporate chef, and a corporate jet with six pilots and its own hangar. All this, though the company had been losing money for years. The system was broken.

Fortunately, Maggie Wilderotter is smart, confident, and deeply empathetic—a natural leader. I work with her on the boards of Okta and Lyft and those companies' CEOs don't have to be told to pay close attention to everything Maggie says. It's just obvious.

When Wilderotter arrived at Frontier, she told me, "Everybody wanted to show me the org chart, to make sure I understood the pecking order. I didn't even look at it, because I believe that work gets done through the go-to people. They may not have titles and positions, but they're the ones who get the work done."

She went on a listening tour of the company and its far-off markets to find out how things were actually run and who those go-to people were. As she put together her strategy, they—not the top executives—were the ones she consulted. She asked the employees what they loved about the company and what they hated. Finally, she spent time thinking about how to dismantle the hierarchy and close the communications gap between the white- and blue-collar workers.

She began by firing her most lackluster executives. She

fired the doctor, the chef, and the six pilots. She sold the hangar and the corporate jet and became the only Fortune 500 CEO at the time who flew commercial. And she gave all the employees their first raise in five years.

Her message was "We're all in this together," but she knew she had to back those words with actions to make them stick. To change the dynamic, Wilderotter arbitrarily took the side of the front line over leadership in every dispute. The details of the disputes mattered less than the principle of giving the workers a voice. If someone in leadership reacted poorly to the idea that the workers on the front lines—and, by extension, the customers they represented—were always right, that person's tenure at Frontier would be short.

But just because Wilderotter began by siding with those on the front lines, to shift the overall dynamic, didn't mean that they were always right.

> People in the local markets would tell me, "I'm not allowed to install the service properly in a way that will satisfy the customer." I would ask, "What do you need?" And they would say, "I don't have the tools to do my job"—meaning literally hammers and screwdrivers. So I'd tell them to go down to the hardware store and buy the tools they needed and give their tech supervisor the bill. The idea was to encourage them to stop complaining and start taking ownership.

That was a good start, but to really make a difference, Wilderotter had to address the union contract. Like many such contracts, it was negotiated between the company's lawyers and the union heads with no management involvement. Because she'd never worked at a company with unions, she questioned why the negotiations had to be done that way:

> We had a very adversarial relationship with our union. The lawyers at corporate would fly around the country and be assholes and do this win-lose thing. The union members worked for the general managers in Connecticut, so I said the general managers should negotiate directly with their employees. And the result was that union members, the people who were installing phones and repairing them, ended up with compensation packages like everyone else: they got profit sharing and stock options. In exchange, they gave on things like healthcare copays. Having shared goals and targets helped make us all one company, helped build this circle of trust. The union guys started to say, "Wow, we can actually make this job and this company better! We can win."

"We're all in this together" had to be a two-way street. Frontier began offering premium television and pay-per-view options to compete with the cable companies. But after it acquired some of Verizon's assets, Frontier discovered that 46 percent of its former Verizon employees subscribed to cable instead of using Frontier's product.

I said to those former Verizon employees, "We have to collectively win in these markets. I bought you because you have great assets, and one of the best assets is all of you in this room. But let me make it perfectly clear who the enemy is. The enemy is not us, it's the cable guys. I know 46 percent of you write a check to the cable guys every month, and I will tell you I'm not signing that check anymore. You've got thirty days to disconnect your cable and convert to our services or you're fired." There was, like, this rumbling. And I said, "We're all in this together, but you need to decide where your loyalties are. They're either to us and to all of you having jobs, secure jobs that I can continue to fund, or they're not. So pick a side. Because on day thirty-one, if you're still a cable subscriber, you don't work here anymore."

Almost all of the employees made the switch. Those who didn't were indeed fired. Those who did became part of Wilderotter's new meritocracy.

The cultural changes took years to accomplish, but they produced exceptional results. In the eleven years that Wilderotter ran Frontier, the union never went on strike. And the company transformed itself from a weird, sleepy, regional Baby Bell that made $3 billion a year into a national broadband provider with operations in twenty-nine states and revenues in excess of $10 billion.

By tearing down the caste system, Wilderotter built intense loyalty among Frontier's employees and freed them

to do their best work. Her approach earned her the nick-
name *the CEO of the People*.

MASTERING INCLUSION—SEEING PEOPLE

Inclusion is a huge and complex issue, and I am not qual-
ified to address all the societal issues associated with
it. So I will focus on how you can apply Genghis Khan's,
Don Thompson's, and Maggie Wilderotter's principles
to give your company a competitive advantage—the advantage of acquiring the best talent available. All three
understood more than just national or racial or gender
diversity; they also understood cognitive and cultural
diversity—people's disparate and unique ways of processing information, thinking, and interacting with others. By seeing people for who they were they could see
what they truly had to offer.

There were three keys to Genghis Khan's approach to
inclusion:

1. He was deeply involved in the strategy and implemen-
   tation, down to having his own mother adopt children
   from a conquered tribe to symbolize the integration process.
2. He started with the job description he needed to fill,
   be it cavalry, doctors, scholars, or engineers, and then
   went after the talent to fill it. He did not assume that
   every person with a particular background could do
   the job that people with similar backgrounds had

done—that all Chinese officials would make great administrators.

3. Not only did he make sure that conquered people were treated equally, but through adoption and intermarriage, he made them kin. They weren't brought into the empire under some separate but supposedly equal side program. As a result, they felt truly equal—and became more loyal to him and to the Mongols than to their original clans.

Compare this to modern companies where:

1. CEOs delegate inclusion programs to "heads of diversity."

2. These heads of diversity are tasked with achieving diverse representation rather than with the whole company's success. So they often focus on achieving specific race and gender targets rather than on finding talent from diverse pools.

3. Companies often outsource integration to hired diversity consultants who have no understanding of the company's business objectives. That is, the companies make no further efforts to turn themselves into a great place to work for their new hires. As a result, while hiring numbers show progress, the real story lies in employee satisfaction numbers and the attrition rate of new hires. The first will be low, the second high.

If the key to inclusion means seeing someone for who they are even if they come in a color or gender that you're not used to, then it follows that hiring people on the basis of color or gender will actually defeat your inclusion program. You won't see the person, you will just see the package.

This seems obvious enough, but it's actually trickier to understand than it would seem, because if you are hiring your own race or gender then you can see them just fine. If a woman hires a woman, there will probably be no problem later. If a man does it, then he runs a strong chance that he'll only see that she's a woman and not who she really is. Because most advisors on inclusion come from the groups being included, they often miss this point. And this is why hiring women and minorities into senior positions usually accelerates your inclusion efforts.

Good intentions, pursued without meticulous forethought and follow-through, often lead to catastrophe. A few years ago, my friend Steve Stoute and I were discussing his career in the music industry, a relatively integrated field. He was reminiscing about his time as president of Sony Urban Music, and he went off on how ridiculous his title was. He said, "They couldn't call me president of Black Music, because that would be offensive, so they called it Urban Music. But that's not even the real problem. Since we called it 'Urban Music,' I was only allowed to market in cities—as if no black people lived out in the country." He went on to say that even calling it "black music" wouldn't have helped: "We had Michael Jackson. What white people don't like Michael Jackson? It's not black music; it's *music*."

Many companies fall short of Genghis Khan's standard by implementing a sort of *Urban HR*. They set up the diversity department as though female talent, African-American talent, and Hispanic talent are fundamentally different from white talent, male talent, or Asian talent. If you only listen to music from one race then you probably do not understand music. If you only hire talented people from one race or gender, then you probably do not understand talent. I know this because until recently I did not understand talent.

A few years after we started Andreessen Horowitz, I looked at the makeup of our organization and of other top companies in tech. The pattern was clear. Every organization tended to resemble the person in charge. If a woman ran the company, women were overrepresented. If a Chinese-American person ran engineering, you'd find lots of Chinese-American engineers. If an Indian-American ran marketing, there'd be Indian-Americans all over the marketing department. Why? It all started with the hiring profile. People understand their own strengths, value them highly, and know how to test for them in an interview.

Our firm had this issue in every department. Our head of marketing was a woman and she had a lot of women working for her. I asked her what was in her profile that made it difficult for men to get a job in marketing. "Helpfulness," she replied. I was floored. Of course! We were a services firm. Every job description in our company should have helpfulness in the profile, but I was the founder and I had never even considered it. I was blind. I could not see the exact contours of the talent we needed to find, so we were missing out.

People who come from different backgrounds and cultures bring different skills, different communication styles, and different mores to the organization. When we tested for helpfulness, women scored higher (though of course there are helpful men, too). Testing for it required me to think differently about how we assess candidates. One thing to look for is volunteer work, which helpful people naturally like to do. It also turns out that during the interview, helpful people want to talk much more about the interviewer than about themselves: by learning about her they can anticipate her needs and be, well, helpful.

Similarly, when we tested for the ability to create a relationship, African-Americans scored higher. We'd look for it by seeing how candidates built relationships with us during the interview—after interviewing someone, did you want to spend more time with him? One young African-American man who was great at it turned out to have the highest tips of any Cheesecake Factory waiter in the nation. He was absolutely expert at creating an instantaneous relationship. If you're having trouble seeing the value in a particular talent pool, the answer is not to set up a parallel talent process for those groups; the answer is to fix the talent process you have so you can cure your blindness.

I knew we had to change our selection process if we wanted to compete at the highest level. Like many companies, our recruiting networks emanated from our employees. So we had to broaden our talent network. To build our African-American talent network, for instance, we held events with prominent African-American leaders such as Bernard Tyson (CEO, Kaiser Permanente), Judy Smith (the crisis manager who inspired the show *Scandal*), and Ken Coleman (a leading Silicon Valley executive), and reached out to African-American tech organizations such as /dev/color, NewMe, and the Phat Startup.

Next, we changed our hiring process. When a manager wants to make a new hire, she must now have people from talent pools different from her own (for instance, U.S. military veterans, African-Americans, etc.) review the hiring criteria and make suggestions about what they would hire for and how they would test for those qualities. For example, one criterion men often overlook when hiring a manager—but women rarely do—is the ability to give feedback. Women are more willing to confront a co-worker and have a difficult conversation; men often avoid the issue until it gets superhot. We also made sure that our interview teams came from a range of backgrounds, so that we were better able to see the complete candidate.

Our new process is not perfect, but it is clearly better than our old one. Today half of our 172 people are women, and the firm is 27 percent Asian and 18.4 percent African American and Hispanic. That's a lot of talent that we might not have seen had we stuck to our old process.

More important, we haven't just improved our numbers. We've improved our cultural cohesion. Because we test for helpfulness, we value it and we value the people who have it. We can see them for who they are, not what they look like.

It's easy to value the things that you test for in an interview and nearly impossible to value things that you don't. When a company hires an African-American employee because he or she is African-American, then race becomes a reason for making decisions in that culture and the culture often becomes racist. What you do is who you are. If someone enters a company through the Urban HR division, everyone will remember that fact, and the employee will be suspect and have to prove herself over and over. Whereas if everyone is hired on the same criteria, then the culture will see people for who they are and what they uniquely bring to the table.

8 BE YOURSELF, DESIGN YOUR CULTURE

I don't want you to be me, you should just be you.
—*Chance the Rapper*

The first step in getting the culture you want is knowing what you want. It sounds obvious and it is; it sounds easy, but it's not. With seemingly infinite possibilities to choose from, how do you design a culture that gives your organization the advantages it needs, creates an environment you are proud of, and that—most importantly—can actually be implemented?

A few points to keep in mind:

- Whether your company is a startup or a hundred years old, designing your culture is always relevant. Cultures, like the organizations that create them, must evolve to meet new challenges.

- All cultures are aspirational. I have worked with

thousands of companies and none of them ever achieved total cultural compliance or harmony. In a company of any significant size there will always be violations. The point is not to be perfect, just better than you were yesterday.

- While you can draw inspiration from other cultures, don't try to adapt another organization's ways. For your culture to be vibrant and sustainable, it must come from the blood, from the soul.

BE YOU

Step one in designing a successful culture is to be yourself. That's not so easy.

In 1993, the basketball player Charles Barkley famously said, "I am not a role model. Just because I dunk a basketball doesn't mean that I should raise your kids." Many people thought this statement was clever, and it led to a Nike ad campaign. After the campaign became wildly popular, a reporter asked Barkley's teammate Hakeem Olajuwon if he, too, was "not a role model." Olajuwon replied, "I am a role model."

Olajuwon explained that Charles Barkley was one person in private and a totally different person in public. As maintaining a dual personality was extremely stressful, he said, Barkley was constantly looking for a way out. Because he did not feel he was really the person the NBA wanted him to be, when he went out partying, he did it to the extreme. Olajuwon said that he himself was the opposite: exactly the same in public and private. As a result, he was indeed a role model.

This interview revealed a key to leadership: you *must* be yourself. Other people will always have ideas of what you should be, but if you try to integrate all those ideas in a way that's inconsistent with your own beliefs and personality, you will lose your mojo. If you try to be someone else, not only will you be unable to lead, but you'll be ashamed to have people emulate you. In essence, Charles Barkley was saying, "Don't follow me. Even *I* don't like me."

Under the spotlight, managers find it very hard to just be themselves. Say that an excellent coworker, Stan, gets his first promotion to manager. All his colleagues are excited. But then Stan becomes "Manager Stan"— and magically transforms into a dick. Because he feels he has to establish his authority, he stops treating you like a person and starts treating you like someone he has to impress with his power. Nobody likes or respects Manager Stan.

At the CEO level, this issue plays out more subtly. Many CEOs model a successful leader whose methods they haven't internalized or whose best practices don't apply to their company. For example, a CEO might read about Jack Welch's "rank and yank" process, where he ranked all the General Electric employees and eliminated the lowest performers. The CEO decides to do the same—look how well it worked for Jack! When he brings the idea to his managers, one says, "But we have this super-intense hiring process where we're only allowed to hire the very top people in the industry. Our bottom ten percent is pretty darned good." The CEO thinks, That's right. In fact, I set up that process.

Now the CEO is in a bind. Does he stick to his guns even though he doesn't really believe in his idea anymore? Or does he risk looking wishy-washy by reversing himself on the spot? This is a no-win—all because he wanted to be Jack Welch. If you aren't yourself, even *you* won't follow you.

A CEO will often hear something like this from a board member: "I don't think your CFO is as good as the CFOs of other companies whose boards I'm on." This is an extremely tricky statement to deal with. The CEO doesn't know those other CFOs, and she can't interview them and compare. How does she respond? The CEO's common—and wrong—move is to go tell her CFO to be better in front of the board. She is trying to be what the board member wants, but failing, because she has refused to have a point of view. Her CFO will be confused, because he has no idea what he's done wrong. He will try to transform into something he's not and also lose his leadership mojo.

The CEO should tell the board member, "Great. Let me know what you think makes those CFOs better than our guy, and please introduce me to them." The CEO should spend time with those CFOs, decide for herself whether she comes to the same assessment of a skills gap, then— and this step is critical—decide how important those skills are for her company. If the skills are vital and the difference in skills between her CFO and the external

CFOs is real, she can go back to her CFO, tell him where he stands, and let him know that he's not going to make it. She can be herself. If she disagrees with the board member, she can be herself with him, too. And she'll have done the work to back up her response.

If you follow the first rule of leadership, not everybody will like you. But trying to get everybody to like you makes things even worse. I know this, because not everybody likes me. In fact, I am sure someone reading this right now is saying, "Who does that old white dude think he is quoting Chance the Rapper?" I am okay with that. I don't want to be cool. I just want to be me.

BUT KNOW WHICH PARTS OF YOU NEED WORK

There are parts of any CEO's personality that he doesn't actually want in the company. Think carefully about what your flaws are, because you don't want to program them into your culture—or else leading by example will bite you in the ass.

One part of my personality that didn't work so well in a software company was my willingness to engage in endless, unstructured conversation. (That habit is a better fit at a venture capital firm.) Tip to my future friends: if you don't end our phone calls we might literally talk forever.

When you need a large organization to work in concert and execute with precision on an enormous number of tasks, you simply don't have time to explore every nook and cranny of every issue in every conversation.

So my discursiveness—which I still like to think of as curiosity—could be extremely disadvantageous. I learned to counterprogram the culture against my inclinations in three ways:

1. I surrounded myself with people who had the opposite personality trait. They wanted to finish the conversation as soon as possible and move on to the next thing.
2. I made rules to help manage myself. If a meeting was called without a tightly phrased written agenda and a desired outcome, we'd cancel it.
3. I announced to the company that we were committed to running meetings efficiently—talking the talk that I did not like walking, and forcing myself to walk it as much as I could.

The company still suffered from my inefficient personal style, but we were mostly able to work around it.

APPLYING WHO YOU ARE

Once you're comfortable with who you are, you can begin to map that identity onto the culture you want. When Dick Costolo took over as CEO of Twitter, his advisor Bill Campbell joked that if you set off a bomb at 5 p.m., only the cleaning people would get killed. Costolo wanted to change the culture to encourage hard work. Costolo himself is a grinder. After having dinner with his family every night, he'd go back to work and make himself available to anyone who was still there and who wanted to get something done that needed his help. Pretty soon, a lot of people were working longer hours and getting more done. If Costolo wasn't the type of person who could focus and be effective for very long hours, his plan never would have worked.

It is much easier to *walk the talk* when the talk is your natural chatter. When I was a young manager, written feedback had a much greater impact on me than verbal feedback (even though I was obviously fond of chatting). I liked writing my own reports. As CEO of Opsware it made sense to me that written feedback would be a vital part of our culture. If I hated writing, that virtue would never have worked.

A company's culture needs to reflect the leader's sensibilities. No matter how much you want a learning environment or a frugal company or a place where everyone works late, you will not get one unless that is what you instinctively do yourself. If the expressed culture goes one way but you walk in the opposite direction, the company will follow you, not your so-called culture.

CULTURE AND STRATEGY. DID SOMEBODY SAY BREAKFAST?

The management consultant Peter Drucker famously said: "Culture eats strategy for breakfast." It is a great line and I love it, but I disagree with it. I love it, because it is marvelously anti-elitist: *Screw what the executive suite says, what matters is what the people are doing.* That's totally correct. I also love that Drucker's observation elevates culture to a high-order consideration. But the truth is that culture and strategy do not compete. Neither eats the other. Indeed, for either to be effective, they must cohere.

Genghis Khan's military strategy called for nearly everyone to play the same role: a self-sufficient cavalry soldier. So his egalitarian culture perfectly fit his strategic needs. When Shaka Senghor's strategy was to have a smaller but more elite gang than his competitors, he built his culture around a camaraderie that the larger gangs couldn't match.

When Jeff Bezos created Amazon's long-term strategy, a key element was a lower cost structure. So a cultural attentiveness to frugality made perfect sense.

For a company like Apple, whose strategy depended on building the most beautiful, perfectly designed products in the world, frugality would have been counterproductive. In fact, John Scully nearly destroyed the company when he fired Steve Jobs for, in part, his lack of cost consciousness. Not every virtue fits every strategy.

If you want to create strategic advantage by being the fastest-innovating company in the world, then Facebook's original motto, "Move fast and break things," makes perfect sense. If you are Airbus, making airplanes, it might not be such a good idea.

Pick the virtues that will help your company accomplish its mission.

SUBCULTURES

This book would be much more elegant if I could just assert that all companies have a single, cohesive, non-conflicting culture. Alas, any company of any significant size will have subcultures in addition to its main culture.

Subcultures usually emerge because the divisions of a company are often quite distinct from one another. As different functions require different skill sets, salespeople, marketing people, HR people, and engineers tend to come from different schools, to have majored in different subjects, and to have different personality types. This leads to cultural variation.

In tech, the most pronounced difference is between sales and engineering. As an engineer, you need to know how things work. If you're asked to build a new function for an existing product, you must understand precisely how that product works. So you often have to talk to the code's author, who must be able to tell you exactly how she designed it and how all of its components interact. People who are abstract, nonlinear, or imprecise in their communication have difficulty fitting into engineering organizations, because they leave bugs in their wake.

As a salesperson, you must know the truth. Does the customer have the necessary budget? Are you ahead of or behind the competition? Who in the target organization is a supporter and who is a detractor? Experienced salespeople like to say, "Buyers are liars." That's because, for a variety of reasons, buyers do not volunteer the truth. They may enjoy being wined and dined; they may be using you as a stalking horse to get a better price out of the competition; or they may just have a hard time saying "No." Like Jack Bauer in *24* interrogating a terrorist, you must extract the truth. In sales, if you take what you're told at face value, you won't last.

When you ask an engineer a question, her instinct is to answer it with great precision. When you ask a salesperson a question, she'll try to figure out the question behind the question. If a customer asks, "Do you have feature X?" a good engineer will answer yes or no. A good salesperson will almost never answer that way. She will ask herself, "Why are they asking about that feature? Which competitor has that feature? Hmm, then they must be in the account trying to take my deal. I need more information." So she'll reply with something like, "Why do you think feature X is important?"

Having their questions answered with questions drives engineers insane. They want answers fast, so they can get back to work. But if they hope to see their product succeed—if they want great salespeople to go sell it, so they can keep working for a company that's still in business—they need to be able to tolerate that cultural difference.

In a well-run organization, engineers get compensated more for how good the product is than for how much money it ends up bringing in, because there are often serious market risks that are outside the engineer's control. Great engineers love to build things and often code on side projects as a hobby. So creating a comfortable environment that encourages round-the-clock programming is vital. Hallmarks of engineering cultures often include casual dress, late morning arrival times, and late or very late evening departure times.

Great salespeople are more like boxers. They may enjoy what they do, but nobody sells software on the weekends for fun. Like prizefighting, selling is done for the money and the competition—no prize, no fight. So sales organizations focus on commissions, sales contests, president's clubs, and other prize-oriented forms of compensation. Salespeople represent the company to the outside world, so they need to dress accordingly and show up early, when their customers punch in. Great sales cultures are competitive, aggressive, and highly compensated—but only for results.

While every company needs core common cultural elements, trying to make all aspects of your culture identical across functions means weakening some functions in favor of others. For example, virtues like "We are obsessed with customers," "The best idea wins regardless of rank," and "We outwork the competition" all apply at the company level. But "We dress casually" or "We only care about results" are usually more apt for a subculture.

A SPECIFICATION FOR EMPLOYEES

One way to think about designing your culture is to conceive it as a way to specify the kinds of employees you want. What virtues do you value most in employees? Making your virtues precisely the qualities you're looking for in an employee reinforces an important concept from bushido: virtues must be based on actions rather than beliefs. Because, trust me, it's really easy to fake beliefs in an interview. If you hire for what people can do, on the other hand, you can find out through reference checks if they've done it in the past, and you can even test for it in the interview.

Making your hiring profile a big part of how you define your culture makes enormous sense—because who you hire determines your culture more than anything else. Patrick Collison, cofounder and CEO of Stripe, told me:

> Honestly, most of what ultimately defined us happened in the hiring of the first twenty people. So the question of what do you want the culture to be and who do you want to hire are in some sense the same question.

Stewart Butterfield, the cofounder and CEO of Slack, said that orienting his culture around the kind of employees he wanted has started to dramatically improve things at the company:

> Our values were really original—they included playfulness and solidarity, for instance—but they weren't an effective guide to action. We were trying to find something that would help people make a decision.
>
> Then I remembered a conversation I had with Suresh Khanna, who led sales at AdRoll. One thing he said really stuck with me. He said that when he was recruiting he looked for people who were smart, humble, hardworking, and collaborative.

That's what we needed. Those four are especially valuable in combination, because if you have just two of the four it can be a disaster. If I tell you someone is smart and hardworking, but neither humble nor collaborative, that's going to bring an archetype to mind and it's not a good one. Same with someone who is humble and collaborative but isn't smart or hardworking. You know that person and you don't want them.

His ideas about what makes a good employee or candidate were much more actionable than ours—it's hard to measure someone's playfulness or solidarity in an interview. I began looking for these four:

1. *Smart.* It doesn't mean high IQ (although that's great), it means disposed toward learning. If there's a best practice anywhere, adopt it. We want to turn as much as possible into a routine so we can focus on the few things that require human intelligence and creativity. A good interview question for this is: "Tell me about the last significant thing you learned about how to do your job better." Or you might ask a candidate: "What's something that you've automated? What's a process you've had to tear down at a company?"

2. *Humble.* I don't mean meek or unambitious, I mean being humble in the way that Steph Curry is humble. If you're humble, people want you to succeed. If you're selfish, they want you to fail. It also gives you the capacity for self-awareness, so you can actually learn and be smart. Humility is foundational like that. It is also essential for the kind of collaboration we want at Slack.

3. *Hardworking.* It does not mean long hours. You can go home and take care of your family, but when you're here, you're disciplined, professional, and focused. You should also be competitive, determined, resourceful, resilient, and gritty. Take this job as an opportunity to do the best work of your life.

4. *Collaborative.* It's not submissive, not deferential—in fact it's kind of the opposite. In our culture, being collaborative means providing leadership from everywhere. I'm taking responsibility for the health of this meeting. If there's a lack of trust, I'm going to address that. If the goals are unclear, I'm going to deal with that. We're all interested in getting better and everyone should take responsibility for that. If everyone's collaborative in that sense, the responsibility for team performance is shared. Collaborative people know that success is limited by the worst performers, so they are either going to elevate them or have a serious conversation. This one is easy to corroborate with references, and in an interview you can ask, "Tell me about a situation in your last company where something was substandard and you helped to fix it."

Someone with strength in all four attributes is the perfect Slack employee.

Once you have your specification for employees clearly established, how do you apply it? Amazon selected people to serve as *the Bar Raiser.* Their function in interviews is to test candidates on their ability to understand

Amazon's leadership principles and fit into its culture. Crucially, the person who is the Bar Raiser is not on the hiring team and has no vested interest in the candidate—his or her mission is purely cultural. Prioritizing this role does two things. First, it establishes a strong test of cultural fit. Second, and perhaps more important, it sends a message to every candidate that Amazon's culture is vitally important.

A well-designed cultural interview need not be long. Parametric Technology Corporation (PTC) is a computer-aided-design software company with a legendary sales culture. My head of sales at Opsware, culture-changer Mark Cranney, came from PTC and was always bragging about how good they were at selling. I got annoyed and asked why they were so great. He said, "Well, it started with the interview. I walked into the interview with the senior vice president of sales, John McMahon. He said nothing for what seemed like five minutes, then asked me, 'What would you do if I punched you in the face right now?'"

At this point in Mark's story, I cried, "What!? He wanted to know what you would do if he punched you in the face? That's crazy. What did you say?"

Mark said, "I asked him, 'Are you testing my intelligence or my courage?' And McMahon said, 'Both.' So I said, 'Well, you'd better knock me out.' He said, 'You're hired.' Right then I knew that I'd found a home."

How did McMahon make a hiring decision so quickly? That brief exchange enabled him to suss out whether Mark was a fit with his key cultural elements: the ability to keep your poise under fire, the ability to listen carefully, the courage to discover why a question is being asked—and, most of all, competitiveness.

A UNIVERSAL ELEMENT OF STRONG CULTURES— WHAT YOU DO MUST MATTER

While you should design your culture to meet the unique needs of your organization, there is one element every company needs. Almost no one ever makes it part of their stated set of values, but it's impossible to build a winning company without it.

The questions employees everywhere ask themselves all the time are "Will what I do make a difference? Will it matter? Will it move the company forward? Will anybody notice?" A huge part of management's job is to make sure the answer to all those questions is "Yes!"

The most important element of any corporate culture is that people care. They care about the quality of their work, they care about the mission, they care about being good citizens, they care about the company winning. So a gigantic portion of your cultural success will be determined by what gets rewarded at your company. Is it caring about your work? Or do you do better financially if you actually give zero fucks? Every time an employee works hard to make a change or to propose a new idea only to be met with bureaucracy, indecision, or apathy, the culture suffers. Every time an employee is recognized or rewarded for pushing the company forward, the culture strengthens.

When HP acquired Opsware in 2007, I became a general manager at HP Software. Walking in as an outsider, I set out to meet as many employees as I could one-on-one. Very soon a pattern emerged—nobody seemed to care about what he or she did. People didn't care to the point where employees couldn't get the simplest answers to questions like "Can I make this hire?," "Can I pick the tool that I will use to develop this software?," or "Can I get a new cover for the fluorescent light that's glaring down on my cube?"

At HP people were rewarded for not caring. The company had gone through a series of brutal cost-cutting measures that produced spectacular short-term earnings but decimated the culture. Many people "worked from home" but did not actually work at all. When the company changed leaders in 2010, the new CEO was startled to learn that there were 15,000 fewer chairs in the company than employees in its head count—15,000 people never came to work and nobody had noticed. The people who did come to work and who worked hard were punished with indecision and further rounds of cost cutting.

I remember thinking, If I can't get these simple questions decided, why would anyone even bother coming to work? So I made every employee in my several-thousand-person organization a promise: "If you have an issue and you need a decision and you cannot get one from your manager, send it to me and I will get you a decision in one week." A small gesture, but it created an immediate change in attitude from the best employees. In just a few weeks we went from a "can't do" culture to a "can do" culture.

I'd like to say that this led to a rebirth of HP, but it did not. After years of having been a CEO, I discovered that I could no longer work for someone else. I left the company less than a year later and it became what it became—a company that eventually had to be broken up into smaller components to regain its mojo.

If your organization can't make decisions, can't approve initiatives quickly, or has voids where leadership should be, it doesn't matter how many great people you hire or how much work you spend defining your culture. Your culture will be defined by indifference, because that's what you're rewarding. If I work hard and my neighbor does nothing and we both have the same impact at the company, then her behavior is obviously the way to go.

ATTRIBUTES THAT MAKE CULTURAL VIRTUES EFFECTIVE

Many potential cultural elements are too abstract to be effective. If you define "integrity" as a virtue, will that clarify exactly how people should behave? If there's a conflict, does integrity mean meeting your product schedule as promised or delivering the quality that your customers expect?

Some ways of thinking about a virtue's effectiveness:

- *Is your virtue actionable?* According to bushido, a culture is not a set of beliefs, but a set of actions. What actions do your cultural virtues translate to? Can you turn empathy, for instance, into an action? If so, it may work as a virtue. If not, best to design your culture with a different virtue.
- *Does your virtue distinguish your culture?* Not every virtue will be unique to your company, but if every other business in your field does the same thing, there is probably no need to emphasize it. If you're a Silicon Valley company, there is no need to make casual dress a virtue, because that's the default behavior. But if you're a technology company and you want everyone to wear a suit and tie, that will define your culture.
- *If you are tested on this virtue, will you pass the test?*

Todd McKinnon, the CEO of Okta, got tested on his most important cultural tenet early in his tenure.

Prior to cofounding Okta in 2009, McKinnon was a vice president of engineering at Salesforce.com. Okta provided a secure identity system for companies that had moved their applications to the cloud. Hosting applications on the cloud was a new idea at the time, but having seen Salesforce explode, McKinnon felt that there would be many more such applications to come—marketing automation, legal apps, customer support, and so on. Cloud-based companies would then face the challenge of managing their employees' activities across hundreds of systems they didn't own. If you fire an employee, how can you be sure you've removed her from every system she had access to? This was the initial problem Okta sought to address.

Every customer would have to trust Okta to manage the credentials of all their employees across hundreds and perhaps thousands of systems. If Okta went down, even for maintenance, those employees wouldn't be able to access their vital data. Even worse, if Okta got hacked, all their customers would also be hacked. As Okta had to be totally trusted to succeed, McKinnon had to make integrity the core of the culture.

But Okta was a startup. And the prime cultural virtue of any startup is *survive at all costs*. About three years in, Okta was struggling; it had missed seven forecasts in a row and needed to raise money. A potential large deal with Sony would make or break the quarter. The good news was that the deal was on track. The bad news was that Okta's sales rep had promised Sony that a feature called on-premise user provisioning—which would allow Sony to put users into the system from within its own buildings—would be delivered in a few months. In fact, Okta didn't plan to build it for a few years. Sony didn't require contractual assurance that the feature was just around the corner, but it did want McKinnon's word. Was the smart thing to do to tell Sony the truth, or was it to save the company? Was that feature so important to Sony that it had to be warned that it would be delivered a little late—even at the risk of layoffs at Okta, or worse?

"I knew that I could get the deal if I stretched the truth," McKinnon recalled. "But I knew that everyone from the sales rep to the engineers would know that I had done that. They would assume that little lies were okay. I'd like to say it was an easy decision, but it was a hard decision. I ended up not taking the deal, because I knew it would be fatal in the long run. And maybe more than that because I did not want to lie."

He chose to risk the company rather than risking the culture. In this case, it worked out. Khosla Ventures made a gutsy bet and funded Okta's next round despite all those missed quarters. As of this writing, Okta is worth nearly $15 billion and has become the most important cloud-identity product in the world. Okta has still never been hacked and its uptime is legendary—it has gone as much as four years with no downtime.

But Todd's decision could just as easily have finished the company. And then nobody would even remember Okta or the courage he showed.

Your employees will test you on your cultural virtues, either accidentally or on purpose, so before you put one into your company, ask yourself, "Am I willing to pass the test on this?"

9 EDGE CASES AND OBJECT LESSONS

> You're quite hostile, I've got a right to be hostile, my
> people been persecuted.
> —*Public Enemy*

To truly grasp how culture works, we need to examine the sticky places where it doesn't. The unmapped terrain out on the boundaries where cultural principles often break down or become counterproductive. When does too much of a good thing become a bad thing? When does following one cultural principle violate another? Is it okay to violate your cultural principles to survive? Do cultural tenets ever run their course and need to be retired?

WHEN CUSTOMER OBSESSION LEADS TO RECESSION

One cultural virtue many companies try to live by is customer obsession. They want to know every want, desire, and whim of their customers, then work relentlessly to satisfy them all. Nordstrom and the Ritz-Carlton built their reputations on this. It's a great value—until it's not. Customers do indeed have strong views about features they'd like in products they already have, but they have fuzzy to nonexistent ideas about products that don't yet exist.

Research In Motion (RIM), which created the Black-Berry in 1999, built a powerful product-based culture in Waterloo, Canada, far from Silicon Valley. It knew its customers better than anyone and it knew that mobile customers valued battery life and keyboard speed above all. RIM also knew that the corporate IT departments that made the buying decisions valued security and integration with existing IT systems. So RIM devoted all its efforts to maximizing those qualities, and for a time it dominated the market.

But this maniacal cultural focus on customers led the company to ignore Apple's iPhone. Why? Because RIM was confident in its incumbency. When the iPhone first appeared it had a lousy battery, a ridiculous keyboard, was integrated into zero IT systems, and had laughable controls for IT to manage security. Who'd want that? That dismissal—that failure of imagination, of cultural flexibility—has shrunk the market cap of BlackBerry Ltd., as the company is now called, from $83 billion to $5 billion.

BREAKING YOUR OWN RULES

Cultural rules can often become bloated sacred cows. Everyone tiptoes around them, trying to respect the culture—and then the cows topple and crush you. Strategies evolve, circumstances change, and you learn new things. When that happens, you must change your culture or you will end up pinned beneath it.

When we founded Andreessen Horowitz, we made a brand promise that became the basis of our culture. We guaranteed that if you raised money from us, the general partner from our firm who'd sit on your board would be a former founder or CEO of a significant tech company. We made that requirement of our general partners because we were determined to be the best place for technical founders—the inventors of this new product, who presumably lacked management experience—to learn how to grow into being a CEO.

To make good on our promise, we also built a powerful platform for giving founders a big-time CEO-like network, connecting them to capital markets, talent, big-company customers, and the press. And we made sure that everyone in the firm had a deep understanding of what a struggle it is to build a company.

We did this through tightly enforced rules about how to treat entrepreneurs, such as being on time for meetings with them, always explaining our reasoning if we chose not to invest, and being honest about our concerns even if that risked the relationship. In keeping with our approach, Marc and I made a rule that we would not promote people to general partner from within the firm. This made total sense at the time, because top founder CEOs weren't interested in our non-GP positions, so anyone we might eventually promote would lack the background we'd promised our portfolio companies.

But as Andreessen Horowitz began to succeed, our perspective changed. We learned that our entrepreneurs valued the capabilities of the firm—our ability to plug them into our network of relationships across big companies, capital markets, the press, and to connect them with executives and engineers they might want to hire— more than our advice. And that some of the former CEOs we hired as GPs had their own views about culture— views that didn't coexist easily with the culture we'd established. They were used to having the company orbit around them, while we needed to have our company orbit around the entrepreneurs.

Meanwhile, our junior people had internalized our culture and become its best evangelists—but some of them were beginning to leave. By not offering them a route to rise to general partner, we were losing not only our best young talent, but our best cultural evangelists. The rule that we put in place to enforce the culture, and marketed hard as our special sauce—I even wrote about it in my book *The Hard Thing About Hard Things*—was actually screwing up the culture.

Many people in the firm knew that the rule had become destructive, but they never told me, because I had publicly wrapped myself in it. I began to realize the problem myself when we hired a young analyst named Connie Chan in 2011. After interviewing her, I told my assistant, Minerva, to find our hiring manager, Frank Chen, right away.

FRANK: What did you think?

BEN: She can definitely do the job. The question is, Does she want to do that job?

FRANK: What do you mean? She's interviewing for that job.

BEN: She's more ambitious than you think.

FRANK: What does that mean?

I got nose to nose with Frank and said, "Just make sure you keep her bowl filled with kibble at all times, because the big dog has got to eat!"

Frank looked at me as though I had lost my mind—but then he made sure to provide Chan with plenty of challenges. One quality I deeply appreciate in Frank is his ability to take a ridiculous instruction like that and run with it.

Why was I so inarticulate? I had seen something in Connie Chan I almost never see. From the comprehensive way she answered every question, to her surgical analysis of the firm, to her total poise, Chan was determined to be the best at everything she did. She was destined for greatness. I saw it, but I could not say it.

I could not say it, because I felt an immediate conflict between her irresistible force and our no-internal-promotion policy. Because we couldn't promote Chan to general partner she'd eventually walk. As she developed over the years, championing spectacular deals like Pinterest and LimeBike, all I could think about was the day she'd leave us. Still, I never thought to change the rule, because it was, well, a rule.

One day our team was reviewing general partner candidates and Jeff Jordan, one of our GPs, said, "I would take Connie over any of these." I said, "But she doesn't meet the criterion." Everyone was silent, but it was a loud silence. Culture is about actions. If the actions aren't working, it's time to get some new ones. We promoted Connie to general partner in 2018 and she is killing it.

Cultural rules aren't always explicit. A few years ago, I was working with a young CEO who believed strongly in his culture. He believed in it so strongly that when his company evaluated its employees, their cultural zeal mattered more than their performance. One day, he told me he wanted to make a personnel change. He said, "My chief marketing officer, Sheila, is an incredible person and the best cultural leader I have. Unfortunately, she comes from a different domain and she really hasn't been able to master our market. It's not her fault, as we thought we'd be in a different business than the one we're in. My plan is to hire a new CMO who knows the domain and move Sheila under her."

I replied, "How much equity does Sheila have? A point? A point and a half?"

"A point and a half."

I said, "If you're a great engineer here and you own one-fifth of a point and you find out the person who *reports* to the head of marketing owns one and a half points, how will you feel? What impact will that have on your culture?"

He frowned, then suggested, "What if I take back some of her equity?"

I said, "Given that her original equity package was fair, how do you think she'd feel about that? Could you expect her to continue here as a great cultural leader?"

He realized that by contorting his chain of command to preserve his culture, he'd wreck it. So he took the hard but necessary decision and fired Sheila—and he provided a glowing reference for her in her next job.

WHEN CULTURE CONFLICTS WITH THE BOARD OF DIRECTORS

An entrepreneur I know, I'll call him Fred, faced a dilemma when his board and his culture clashed. Fred was trying to build trust into the culture, as every CEO should. He knew that without trust his people could not execute—but then he broke his own code and made a promise to an executive without telling his board. He wrote me a note:

> Ben,
>
> I was hoping that you could help with a problem. I verbally promised an exec that I'd give him more equity after our next round of financing but the new investor isn't okay with it. The reasoning by the new board member is fair—the exec is already in the 90th percentile of his compensation range and giving him additional equity just to compensate for the dilution he faces from the new funding round doesn't make sense. I agree with the investor's reasoning and it's the right

policy but feel terrible for going back on my verbal promise. I have learnt the lesson of not promising again, but any advice on fixing the current situation?

Best,

Fred

Very challenging situation. Promising an exec compensation that involves diluting all the other shareholders without consulting the board is bad governance. Worse, Fred was proposing to dilute the person who just invested in his company. On the other hand, if you break a promise to an executive by blaming the board, that will have repercussions not only with the executive, but with everyone he or she tells about being screwed. What to do? I wrote back:

Fred,

I'd give the following speech to the board (or something like it):

I understand and agree with the principle that we should not increase employee compensation every time we have a dilution event. Myself, employees, and investors should all be in the same boat with respect to dilutive events and it would be bad management and bad governance to favor one over another as I have in this case. Furthermore, in this instance, the executive is already well compensated.

However, since I am the one who had the conversation with him, I need to be quite clear. This was not a casual conversation or a possibility—it was a promise. I unequivocally promised him he would get an increase. I know now that was the wrong thing to do, especially without first consulting the board, but I did it.

It is important that each of you understand that this entire company runs on my word and my commitment to keeping it. I make promises to every employee we hire about what kind of company we are and will become. I make promises to existing employees about our chances of succeeding. I make promises to our customers about what we will deliver. Every one of those promises gets replicated by our executives and employees hundreds of times. We make these promises because they are necessary. We cannot build the company without people being able to trust that I will do what I say, because I need the company to act on what I say.

If I violate basic trust with my most highly valued employees, I will break our culture of trust and jeopardize the entire operation. I realize that protecting shareholders is also extremely important, so I propose the following. Either a) I issue the stock increase and reduce the amount of stock available to our other executives by the corresponding amount, or, if you do not trust me to do that, b) The board approves a transfer of my personal stock in the amount of the promised increase to the executive. This issue is that important to me.

Best,

Ben

Fred did as I suggested. But the new board member dug in, the board refused to make the accommodation, and eventually the executive quit.

A disappointing outcome, but for Fred it was instructive. He learned that he needed the right culture on his board as well as in his company. The fact that the new investor cared nothing about the culture of the company—the culture that would to a huge extent determine the fate of his own investment—and cared only about looking like a tough guy would continue to be problematic. Fred ejected the investor. His company continues to grow, bruised but stronger.

TELLTALE SIGNS THAT YOUR CULTURE IS MESSED UP

Determining that your culture is broken is hard. It would be great if you could trust your employees to tell you. But a) they'd need the courage to do that, and b) the person complaining would have to be a good cultural fit themselves or the complaint might actually be a compliment (your culture is working and therefore the complainer, who can't get with the program, doesn't like it), and c) most complaints about culture are too abstract to be useful. The most common complaints that roll up from the ranks (often anonymously) are "Our culture is broken" or "We're not living up to our culture." That may well be true, but it doesn't tell you anything.

So how do you know when you're off track? Here are a few signs:

- *The wrong people are quitting too often.* People quit all the time, but when the wrong people quit for the wrong reasons, it's likely time to make a change. If your business is going well, yet people are leaving at a higher-than-industry-expected rate, you have a culture problem. If they're precisely the people you want to keep, that's an even worse sign. When people selected for their cultural fit don't feel at home it's a particularly bad omen—you picked them for a culture you don't have.
- *You're failing at your top priorities.* Say you're getting deluged with complaints about your customer service, so you make improving it the company's number one priority. After six months, customer satisfaction has improved a little, but basically still sucks. The naive diagnosis is that customer support is broken and you should fire the leader. But customer satisfaction starts with the product, runs through the expectations set by sales and marketing, and finally lands in customer support. So your problem is very likely cultural: your culture does not reward people for delighting customers. Why? Most likely, because it rewards people for making product schedules, hitting the sales number, or producing acclaimed marketing campaigns. You will not be able to fix your customer happiness problem without fixing your culture.
- *An employee does something that truly shocks you.*

Remember Thorston, the lying middle manager? It horrified me to discover that lying was seen, at our company, as acceptable.

To correct that misimpression, I had to fire him. Even so, the object lesson of him getting promoted for lying—which is how people saw it—lingered for years. If you're not careful, the truth can become open to interpretation. Once lines were crossed, our interpretations became loose—as when some of our employees suggested that unguaranteed contracts be counted as bookings—and it was difficult to tighten them back up. If I knew then what I know now, I would have made an all-out effort to reprogram my culture immediately. In addition to firing Thorston, I would have introduced a shocking rule or created an unforgettable piece of lore. I needed an everyday lesson that said, "If you lie to your coworkers, you are fired."

If somebody behaves in a way you can't believe, remember that your culture somehow made that acceptable.

OBJECT LESSONS

No technique more strongly shapes and changes culture than the object lesson. It can seem similar to a shocking rule, but a shocking rule is something you put in place to beg the question of why it's there. No actual situation that invokes the shocking rule has to arise for the rule to have an impact.

An object lesson, by contrast, is a dramatic warning

you put into effect after something bad has happened and you need to correct it in a way that will reset the culture and make sure the bad thing never happens again.

The Chinese general Sun Tzu, author of the oldest military treatise in the world, *The Art of War*, understood object lessons perfectly. The great ancient historian Ssu-ma Ch'ien gives this account of how Sun Tzu employed them:

Sun Tzu Wu was a native of the Ch'i State. Art of War *brought him to the notice of Ho Lu, King of Wu. Ho Lu said to him: "I have carefully perused your 13 chapters. May I submit your theory of managing your soldiers to a slight test?"*

Sun Tzu replied: "You may."

Ho Lu asked: "May the test be applied to women?"

The answer was again in the affirmative, so arrangements were made to bring 180 ladies to the Palace. Sun Tzu divided them into two companies and placed one of the King's favorite concubines at the head of each. He then bade them all take spears in their hands, and addressed them thus: "I presume you know the difference between front and back, right hand and left hand?"

The girls replied: "Yes."

Sun Tzu went on: "When I say 'Eyes front,' you must look straight ahead. When I say 'Left turn,' you must face towards your left hand. When I say 'Right turn,' you must face your right hand. When I say 'About turn,' you must face right round towards the back."

Again the girls assented. The words of command having been thus explained, he set up the halberds and battle-axes in order to begin the drill. Then, to the sound of drums, he gave the order "Right turn." But the girls only burst out laughing. Sun Tzu said: "If words of command are not clear and distinct, if orders are not thoroughly understood, then the general is to blame."

So he started drilling them again, and this time gave the order "Left turn," whereupon the girls once more burst into fits of laughter. Sun Tzu said: "If words of command are not clear and distinct, if orders are not thoroughly understood, then the general is to blame. But if his orders are clear, and the soldiers nevertheless disobey, then it is the fault of their officers."

So saying, he ordered the leaders of the two companies to be beheaded. Now the King of Wu was watching the scene from the top of a raised pavilion; and when he saw that his favorite concubines were about to be executed, he was greatly alarmed and hurriedly sent down the following message: "We are now quite satisfied as to our general's ability to handle troops. If we are bereft of these two concubines, our meat and drink will lose their savour. It is our wish that they shall not be beheaded."

Sun Tzu replied: "Having once received His Majesty's commission to be general of his forces, there are certain commands of His Majesty which, acting in that capacity, I am unable to accept."

Accordingly, he had the two leaders beheaded, and straightway installed the pair next in order as leaders in their place. When this had been done, the drum was sounded for the drill once more; and the girls went *through all the evolutions, turning to the right or to the left, marching ahead or wheeling back, kneeling or standing, with perfect accuracy and precision, not venturing to utter a sound. Then Sun Tzu sent a messenger to the King saying: "Your soldiers, Sire, are now properly drilled and disciplined, and ready for your Majesty's inspection. They can be put to any use that their sovereign may desire; bid them go through fire and water, and they will not disobey."*

But the King replied: "Let our general cease drilling and return to camp. As for us, We have no wish to come down and inspect the troops."

Thereupon Sun Tzu said: "The King is only fond of words, and cannot translate them into deeds."

After that, Ho Lu saw that Sun Tzu was one who knew how to handle an army, and finally appointed him general. In the West, he defeated the Ch'u State and forced his way into Ying, the capital; to the north, he put fear into the States of Ch'i and Chin, and spread his fame abroad amongst the feudal princes. And Sun Tzu shared in the might of the King.

The story sounds superharsh: why kill the concubines? They weren't even soldiers. It seems so unfair. Yet this unfairness was the key to setting the culture Sun Tzu wanted. Because it was so ruthless, he knew the story of the beheadings would travel throughout the kingdom. Nobody would ever be confused about whether it was okay to giggle at an order. This was critical, because Sun Tzu knew that in a battle one soldier losing discipline could cost him everything. He needed the culture to be rock solid from the king to the concubines, and he made it so with a searing object lesson.

If your company faces an existential threat, you may need to employ a similarly unfair object lesson. Imagine you have a rogue salesperson who cuts a side deal with a customer. While the contract states the sale is final, the side letter lets the customer return your product any time during the first three months of the deal. The salesperson never tells finance or legal about the side agreement. The finance department then incorrectly accounts for the sale as revenue, thereby committing accounting fraud (for a sale to be booked as revenue, it cannot be reversible).

What should you do? You certainly have to fire the salesperson and report the accounting error, but will that change the culture? If you don't change the culture, this type of behavior might kill your company, as few companies survive multiple bouts of fraud. The cultural best practice is to take Sun Tzu's approach: you should fire not only the salesperson, but the entire chain of command he reports to. Though managers in sales understand that they're legally responsible for their subordinates' actions, the mass firing will still be wildly unfair to at least some of them. Yet in this situation a CEO must take a Confucian approach, as the needs of the many outweigh the needs of the few. The object lesson will be universally understood: at this company, we never do anything illegal.

If a salesperson merely tells a customer that a feature is coming when it isn't, but he doesn't bind the company to the feature's arrival, then you should reprimand or perhaps fire him, but it won't be necessary to remove the entire hierarchy above him.

DEALING WITH CULTURE BREAKERS

In *The Hard Thing About Hard Things* I wrote a section called "When Smart People Are Bad Employees." These are employees who you think will be incredible, but who turn out to be break the culture. I described the three types of bad employees, all of whom you should probably fire. Below is a digest of what I said—and one additional edge-case type of employee that's more problematic.

The Heretic

Every company needs lots of smart, super-engaged employees who can identify its particular weaknesses and help it improve them. But some employees look for faults not so they can fix them, but so they can build a case. Specifically, a case that the company is hopeless and run by a bunch of morons. The smarter the employee, the more destructive this type of behavior can be—because people are that much more likely to listen to him. He will convince engaged, productive employees to become disengaged and to rally others to do the same. They will question every management decision, break trust, and cause your culture to disintegrate.

Why would a smart person try to destroy the company he works for?

- *He is disempowered.* He feels he can't access the people in charge, so complaining is his only way to get the truth out.
- *He is fundamentally a rebel.* Sometimes these people actually make better CEOs than employees.
- *He is immature and naive.* He cannot comprehend that the people running the company do not know every minute detail of its operations. He therefore believes they are complicit in everything that's broken.

It's very difficult to turn heretics around. Once a heretic takes a public stance, the social pressure to be consistent is enormous. If he tells fifty friends that the CEO is the stupidest person on the planet, reversing that position will cost him enormous credibility. Most people aren't willing to take the credibility hit.

The Flake

Some brilliant people can be totally unreliable. At Opsware, we once hired an undeniable genius—I'll call him Roger. Roger was an engineer in an area where a typical new hire would take three months to become fully productive. Roger came up to speed in two days. On his third day, we gave him a project that was scheduled to take one month. Roger completed the project in three days with nearly flawless quality. More specifically, he completed the project in seventy-two hours. Seventy-two nonstop hours: no breaks, no sleep, no nothing but coding. In his first quarter on the job, he was the best employee that we had and we immediately promoted him.

Then Roger changed. He would miss days of work without calling in. Then weeks of work. When he finally showed up, he apologized profusely, but the behavior didn't stop. His work product also degraded. He became sloppy and unfocused. I could not understand how such a stellar employee could go so haywire. His manager wanted to fire him, because the team could no longer count on Roger for anything. I resisted. I knew that the genius was still in him and I wanted us to find it. We never did. It turns out that Roger was bipolar and had two significant drug problems: 1) he did not like taking his medication and 2) he was addicted to cocaine. Ultimately, we had to fire Roger, but even now, it pains me to think of what might have been.

Flaky behavior often has a seriously problematic cause, from self-destructive streaks to drug habits to moonlighting for other employers. The cultural problem is that if a team is counting on the flake, and she's allowed to flake without explanation, then everyone else on the team believes that he should be able to flake, too.

The Jerk

This smart-bad-employee type can crop up anywhere in the organization, but is particularly destructive at the executive level. At times, most executives can be pricks, dicks, a-holes, or a variety of equally profane nouns. I'd argue that being dramatically impolite can improve clarity or emphasize an important lesson—and anyway, that's not the behavior I'm talking about. I'm talking about someone who looks for an opportunity to attack—the more personal the attack, the better.

Consistently asinine behavior from an executive can cripple a company. As a company grows, its biggest challenge becomes communication. If a member of your staff is a raging jerk, communication can become nearly impossible, because people just stop talking in his vicinity. If whenever anyone brings up a marketing issue the VP of marketing jumps down her throat, guess what topic will never come up?

Soon nobody brings up any topic of any kind when the jerk is in the room—and the entire company slowly degenerates. Note that this dynamic only occurs if the jerk in question is brilliant. Otherwise, nobody will care when he attacks them. The bite only has impact if it comes from a big dog. If one of your big dogs destroys communication on your staff, you need to send him to the pound.

The Prophet of Rage

Sometimes you run into an edge case among your employees whom you may want to consider trying to reform. One special category of the *Jerk* is a type I call the *Prophet of Rage*, in honor of the song by Public Enemy. Prophets are incredibly productive and they have indomitable will. No obstacle is too great, no problem too hard, and they do not care whom they piss off to get the job done. People refer to them as glass breakers, cowboys, toe stompers, and assholes. Really they're just jerks. But often you don't want to get rid of them, because who else is going to do so much high-quality work? You just wish they were easier to work with.

They are so self-righteous it's difficult to even have a conversation with them about the right way to do things, because they believe that if they are doing it, it must perforce be right. Everyone else is always wrong.

Their backgrounds almost never match the typical hiring profile. Often they grew up poor and went to the "wrong" schools. Or they were the "wrong" religion, sexual orientation, or skin color. In one way or another they grew up on the wrong side of the tracks and they believe everybody is judging them on that. They will walk through fire to prove their worth. (This is not to say that everyone with this background is a Prophet of Rage, just that PORs tend to have this background.)

These employees are the corporate version of WMDs. They are the ultimate weapon—but their deployment can be highly destabilizing. How can you prevent them from destroying your culture and possibly your company?

When you manage a POR, you have to keep in mind that they often dish it out much better than they take it. While a POR won't hesitate to viciously attack his peers, the slightest criticism causes him to go into a deep funk. Most managers find such behavior ridiculous and give up when they see it. Most managers therefore forfeit the opportunity for greatness.

PORs are perfectionists. They expect total perfection from themselves and everyone around them. When they see others deliver subpar work or subpar thinking, the prophets become enraged. The same dynamic that enrages them and causes them to stomp on other people's toes makes them recoil at any criticism. As they have dedicated their entire life force to doing great work, any rejection of that work is a personal rejection of them. Keep in mind, too, that a prophet's background will often make him suspect you don't want him there in the first place.

There are three keys to managing PORs:

1. *Don't give feedback on their behaviors, give feedback on their behaviors' counterproductive effect.* If you say, "It is totally unacceptable to scream at people in meetings," the POR will hear, "It's totally unacceptable for *you* to scream at people in meetings, but others can do it all they want, because I am out to get you." Focus instead on how his behaviors were interpreted: "You have a very important mission, but when you screamed at Andy that his team was blocking you, his response wasn't to work harder to unblock you. His reaction was to get you back for embarrassing him in public. Your method was totally ineffective." The POR will initially bristle at the criticism, then realize that you were right, then work extremely hard to fix the problem—because he is, after all, a perfectionist.

2. *Recognize that you can't fix a POR.* No matter how effectively you coach a prophet, you won't completely transform him. So it's better to try to moderate your prophet while letting the rest of the team know that you expect them to accept him due to his incredibly high productivity.

3. *Focus your coaching on what the POR can do.* As your prophet is paranoid, giving entirely negative feedback will only reinforce his life narrative of discrimination. So spend your time working with him on what he *can* do. This will catalyze his superpowers and take your company's production into the stratosphere. For example, if your prophet is a great salesperson who is constantly fighting his peers, challenge him to sell them on his ideas instead of overpowering them.

In the end, the POR must more or less conform to your culture. Be aware that if you try to work with a POR, you will enrage some employees who will bemoan this special treatment: why wasn't the POR fired immediately for his cultural transgressions?

Sometimes this cultural deviance proves to be diversity in disguise. But sometimes cultural cohesion is more important than individual performance and it might be best to let the POR go. Keep in mind that this, too, is a cultural statement: you are saying that regardless of performance, you will not tolerate much deviance.

This raises the deeper-level question of what kind of culture you want. Are you a zero-exception place, or one that tolerates diversity and idiosyncrasy? If you're uncomfortable telling a complaining employee something like "Floyd is a special talent, so we are going to give him a little more time to fit in," then you are a zero-exception culture, and you should not even attempt to deal with PORs.

Even with the best coaching, you may find that your prophet has too much rage to function in your organization as it grows. But it's worth trying hard to harness their energies: a great Prophet of Rage can be the most powerful force your company has.

THE CULTURE OF DECISIONS

The decisions you make influence your culture as much as anything. But the process you use to make those decisions also becomes a core part of your culture.

There are essentially three high-level decision-making styles:

1. *My way or the highway.* This leader says, "I don't care what you all think, we're doing it my way. If you don't like it, the door is right behind you." This is maximally efficient as the decision-making process requires no discussion at all.
2. *Everyone has a say.* This leader favors a democratic process. If he could call for a formal vote on every decision, he would. Decisions take a long time to get made, but everybody is guaranteed a say.
3. *Everyone has input, then I decide.* This leader seeks a balance between getting the right information and using all the brain power available, and keeping the process efficient. Her process is not as empowering as *Everyone has a say* or as efficient as *My way or the highway.*

In business, the third style tends to work best. *My way or the highway* disempowers everyone beneath the CEO and creates severe bottlenecks at the top. *Everyone has a say*, ironically, drives everyone completely nuts—employees dislike it even more than *My way or the highway.*

CEOs are judged on the efficiency of their process and the acuity of their decisions, and *Everyone has input, then I decide* tends to balance informed decision making with speed. It also acknowledges that not everyone in the organization has enough information to make a given decision, so someone has to be in charge of becoming knowledgeable and then deciding how to proceed.

The most common cultural breakdown occurs after the decision has been made. Suppose you decide to cancel a software project. Suppose further that it was primarily a financial decision and the project's manager disagreed. Now the manager has to inform the team. The team, frustrated that all their hard work is being thrown away, will be generally pissed. The natural thing for the manager to say is, "I hear you and, quite frankly, I agree with you, but I was overruled by the powers that be."

This is absolutely toxic to the culture. Everyone on the team will feel marginalized because they work for someone who's powerless. This makes them one level less than powerless. They have just been demoted from the bottom of the totem pole to the ground beneath it. The strong-willed among them will make their displeasure known throughout the company, causing other employees to question the leadership team and to wonder if their own work will ultimately matter. The end result will be apathy or attrition or both.

So it's critical to a healthy culture that whatever your

decision-making process, you insist on a strict rule of *disagree and commit*. If you are a manager, at any level, you have a fundamental responsibility to support every decision that gets made. You can disagree in the meeting, but afterward you must not only support the final decision, you must be able to compellingly articulate the reasons the decision was made.

The manager should have said, "This was a really tough decision. While we have done great work and our project shows real promise, when you consider the overall priorities of the business and where we are with cash, it just does not make sense to continue. We have to focus on our core areas. So, to make sure that everyone on this team is deployed to their highest and best use right now, we have decided to cancel the project." After a major decision like this, it's a good practice to ask employees what they thought of the decision—that way you can find out if the rationale behind the move cascaded down the organization with fidelity. As CEO, I wasn't zero-tolerance about much, but I was definitely zero-tolerance on managers who undermined decisions, because that led to cultural chaos.

The final vital component of the decision-making process is "Do you favor speed or accuracy and by how much?" The answer depends on the nature and size of your business. At a large company like Amazon or General Motors, with tens or hundreds of thousands of employees and thousands of decisions that must be made each day, speed is far more important than accuracy. In many cases, it will often be faster to make the wrong decision, discover that it's wrong, and pivot to the right decision, than to spend the time a priori figuring out the right decision.

Imagine a large company taking six months to decide whether to include a particular feature on the product. That would mean that for six months, one hundred employees might be blocked from making progress on everything related to the product. Was the decision really that critical? Did they really need to debate it for six months? Probably not.

On the other hand, consider a business like Andreessen Horowitz, where I work. We make about twenty important investment decisions a year. Getting those right is generally a much higher priority than making them quickly. If you only have twenty shots on goal in a year, you want to make sure each one counts. So we'll spend hours and hours debating, visiting and revisiting aspects of our decision—then work through the entire process again the next day. Accuracy is much more important to us than speed.

Even if you generally favor speed, it is often important culturally to favor accuracy in certain situations. If "great design" or "great taste" is a key part of your value proposition and your culture, then it might be useful to spend dozens of hours debating the exact shade of black of your product's packaging. Taking such pains might not materially improve your sales, but it will absolutely reinforce the cultural message that you don't take shortcuts about design.

Some decisions are so "make or break" that they require a different process. Amazon generally has a "two-pizza teams" process: there should be no more people making most product decisions than can be fed by two pizzas. However, when Amazon is deciding whether to launch a new cloud service requiring a multibillion-dollar investment, it runs a much longer process with many more people involved.

In the speed-versus-accuracy calibration, the cultural question of empowerment plays an important role. How far down the org chart can a decision get made? Do you trust lower-level employees to decide important matters, and do they have enough information to do so with accuracy?

If employees have a real say in the business, they will be far more engaged and productive. It's also often the case that sending the question up the hierarchy not only slows things down but results in a less accurate decision.

On the other hand, pushing decision making too far down the organization can cause several problems:

- *It can break communication across product groups.* This results in a frustrating customer experience. For years, nearly every Google product had its own customer profile: I might be BenH on gmail, but I couldn't seamlessly log in as BenH on YouTube. This led to a fractured experience for customers and prevented Google from understanding user behavior across its product lines. (Larry Page finally forced his groups to prioritize a common customer profile.)
- *It can break communication between divisions.* Which

can lead to a company making great products that it has no capability to market or sell. Xerox's Palo Alto Research Center (PARC) famously spawned a dizzying array of technological breakthroughs, including the Graphical User Interface, but it could never bring them to market effectively, because the rest of the company didn't understand what they were up to. Eventually, Xerox realized this and spun PARC off as a wholly owned subsidiary.

- *You can lose input from your very best minds.* If you're at Netflix, what decision wouldn't benefit from Reed Hastings's knowledge and experience?

The complexities of all these conflicting imperatives was the subject of a conversation I had with Larry Page in 2012. Page came by my office one day because he was trying to figure out how to organize Google for the future, and he wanted to bounce some ideas off me.

He said he'd just had a conversation with Steve Jobs, who had yelled at him for "doing too many things." Jobs thought Page should focus the company and do a few things really well—just like Apple. Jobs was legendary for being deeply involved in product decisions, and the results were spectacular. Apple's products were beautifully designed, almost magically well integrated, and marketed and sold in a way that felt entirely consistent with the products themselves, right down to how the design of the Apple Store was in harmony with Apple's overall look and feel. In Steve Jobs's world, "doing too many things" was the enemy. How could he apply his best-in-the-world taste or keep his products stunningly well integrated if Apple began experimenting willy-nilly?

I asked Page if he wanted to do a few things really well. He said, "No. If I can't pursue breakthrough ideas, then what's the point of being me?" I said, "Then you need an organizational design and a culture that lets you do that, which is definitely not the Apple way."

We discussed companies that generated a ton of new product directions, such as Thomas Edison's GE, Warren Buffett's Berkshire Hathaway, and Bill Hewlett and Dave Packard's Hewlett-Packard. Page eventually concluded that building out Alphabet, a parent company that contains numerous autonomous companies, including Google, was the right way for him to pursue his goals. Now he is able to pursue everything from human longevity to self-driving cars. But don't expect his ventures to be well integrated with a single design style.

The final consideration in the empowerment-versus-control question is whether you are in peacetime or wartime. Is your business working well and are you focused on creative ways to expand it, or do you face severe existential threats? As I noted in *The Hard Thing About Hard Things*, peacetime and wartime put a CEO in very different modes:

Peacetime CEO knows that proper protocol leads to winning. Wartime CEO violates protocol in order to win. Peacetime CEO focuses on the big picture and empowers her people to make detailed decisions. Wartime CEO cares about a speck of dust on a gnat's ass if it interferes with the prime directive.

Peacetime CEO builds scalable, high-volume recruiting machines. Wartime CEO does that, but also builds HR organizations that can execute layoffs.

Peacetime CEO spends time defining the culture. Wartime CEO lets the war define the culture.

Peacetime CEO always has a contingency plan. Wartime CEO knows that sometimes you gotta roll a hard six.

Peacetime CEO knows what to do with a big advantage. Wartime CEO is paranoid.

Peacetime CEO strives not to use profanity. Wartime CEO sometimes uses profanity purposefully.

Peacetime CEO thinks of the competition as other ships in a big ocean that may never engage. Wartime CEO thinks the competition is sneaking into her house and trying to kidnap her children.

Peacetime CEO aims to expand the market. Wartime CEO aims to win the market.

Peacetime CEO strives to tolerate deviations from the plan when coupled with effort and creativity. Wartime CEO is completely intolerant.

Peacetime CEO does not raise her voice. Wartime CEO rarely speaks in a normal tone.

Peacetime CEO works to minimize conflict. Wartime CEO heightens the contradictions.

Peacetime CEO strives for broad-based buy-in. Wartime CEO neither indulges consensus-building nor tolerates disagreements.

Peacetime CEO sets big, hairy audacious goals. Wartime

CEO is too busy fighting the enemy to read management books written by consultants who have never managed a fruit stand.

Peacetime CEO trains her employees to ensure satisfaction and career development. Wartime CEO trains her employees so they don't get their ass shot off in the battle.

Peacetime CEO has rules like "We're going to exit all businesses where we're not number 1 or 2." Wartime CEO often has no businesses that are number 1 or 2 and therefore does not have the luxury of following that rule.

Switching to wartime mode is easier. As soon as the CEO becomes intensely interested in certain details—beginning to hold daily meetings on production delays, for instance—the company will react quickly and everyone will pick up the wartime mentality.

Going the other way is far more complex. A wartime CEO necessarily becomes a major factor in the overall decision-making process. Even when she doesn't make a given decision, the people who do will use her observations or inferred intentions as a guide. During wartime, the culture of individual empowerment gets diminished.

The transition from wartime CEO Steve Jobs to peacetime CEO Tim Cook dramatically changed Apple's culture around product decisions. Because Cook wasn't nearly as involved as Jobs had been, many of Apple's veterans believed that the company was no longer pursuing excellence with the same intensity. The new culture may prove to have advantages, but it definitely feels like a different place.

Likewise, when Uber switched from Travis Kalanick, a wartime-all-the-time CEO, to Dara Khosrowshahi, a peacetime CEO who simply didn't have the institutional knowledge to make every decision, the company's decision process stalled out until Khosrowshahi could rebuild it. It probably didn't help that he was simultaneously trying to fix the bugs in the old cultural code.

Most CEOs never switch their culture from peacetime to wartime or vice versa. Most CEOs have personalities that are suited for one or the other. Peacetime CEOs tend to be diplomatic, patient, exceptionally sensitive to the needs of their teams, and comfortable giving them lots of autonomy. Wartime CEOs tend to be far more comfortable with conflict, obsessed with their own ideas about the direction of the organization, and almost unbearably impatient and intolerant of anything other than perfection.

So usually, if a change must occur, the board fires the old CEO and brings in someone with the requisite mindset for the new conditions. Google's unintegrated profiles occurred in Eric Schmidt's peacetime regime and weren't fixed until Larry Page took over and restored the company to wartime footing, because he was concerned that it wasn't taking Facebook seriously enough as a competitor. A corollary point is that executives who like working for peacetime CEOs often don't like working for wartime CEOs, and vice versa. Only one executive from Schmidt's staff remains on Page's staff: the inimitable genius David Drummond, who heads up legal and corporate development—and is a self-described chameleon.

10 FINAL THOUGHTS

Got crack all in my drawers, I'm just honest
—*Future*

As we have looked at vital cultures from the samurai and Genghis Khan to a prison gang and Amazon, it should be clear that no one culture is right for everyone. Indeed, no single virtue makes universal sense. Your company's culture should be an idiosyncratic expression of your personality, beliefs, and strategy—and it should keep evolving as your company grows and conditions change.

In this final chapter, I'll dive into three cultural virtues that nearly every organization would do well to have—and examine why they're tricky to implement. Then I'll recap some of the book's most important techniques: your checklist as you launch or reboot your own enterprise.

TRUST

Are you an honest person? I'll bet you thought for a moment, then answered "Yes." Now, who else do you know who's honest? I'll bet that was much harder to answer. How can everyone believe that he or she is honest yet have such difficulty identifying other straight shooters?

The truth about telling the truth is that it doesn't come easy. It's not natural. What's natural is telling people what they want to hear. That makes everybody feel good . . . at least for the moment. Telling the truth requires courage. Less remarked on—but equally important, for our purposes—is that it requires judgment and skill.

Why is it hard for CEOs to be as honest as they'd like? Let's look at a few scenarios:

- Sales are not going well. If you tell your employees the truth, the shrewdest ones will rightly worry about the viability of the company and leave. If they leave, you will continue to miss your numbers, introducing a death spiral of underperformance and attrition.
- Your expense structure is too large and a layoff looms. The company isn't doomed, but if you do a layoff, the press will write that you are. Employees will read that, panic, and leave. And then you really will be doomed.
- An important executive just defected to your biggest competitor because she thinks they have a better product. If you tell the truth about her departure, people will wonder if they should be looking, too.
- The product has a serious flaw that is making your customers turn to your chief competitor. If your employees learn this, they will wonder why they're working for the failing number two company.
- Your last valuation was too high and you're looking at

a down round. Your managers sold new hires on the promise of your stock price going even higher.

In each of these commonplace scenarios, telling the truth seems like committing corporate suicide. Should you just give up and lie? No. Trust derives from candor, and your company will fall apart if your employees don't trust you. The trick—and it's tricky—is to tell the truth without thereby destroying the company.

To do this, you must accept that you can't change reality, but you can assign it a new meaning. Imagine the reality you have to assign meaning to is a layoff. First, recognize that you won't be the only person interpreting the layoff. Reporters will say it means the company has failed. Laid-off employees will feel betrayed and convey that. The employees who remain will have a profusion of interpretations. But if you assign meaning to the layoff before anyone else, and you do so candidly and convincingly, your interpretation has a decent chance of being the one that everyone remembers.

There are three keys to assigning meaning:

1. *State the facts clearly.* "We have to lay off thirty people because we came in four million dollars short of projections"—or whatever the case may be. Don't pretend that you needed to clean up performance issues or that the company is better off without the people you so painstakingly hired. It is what it is and it's important that everyone knows that you know that.

2. *If your leadership caused or contributed to the setbacks*

that necessitated the layoff, cop to that. What was the thinking that led you to expand the company faster than you should have? What did you learn that will prevent you from making that mistake again?

3. *Explain why taking the action you're taking is essential to the larger mission and how important that mission is.* A layoff, done properly, is a new lease on life for the company. It's a hard but necessary step that will enable you to fulfill the prime directive, the mission that everyone signed up for: eventual success. It's your job to make sure that the company didn't lay off those people for no ultimate purpose—something good needs to come of it.

The shining example of assigning meaning was what Abraham Lincoln did in his Gettysburg Address. In explaining to the country why soldiers laid down their lives at Gettysburg, he gave new meaning to the Civil War. And that was a feat. Gettysburg was the bloodiest battle of the bloodiest conflict in American history. The three-day struggle pitted countryman against countryman, brother against brother, and produced some fifty thousand casualties.

At the time, many people understood the Civil War to be about preserving the union or states' rights or the economics of slavery. Lincoln gave it fresh import in a speech so compact and powerful that it's worth reading in its entirety.

Fourscore and seven years ago our fathers brought forth on this continent, a new nation, conceived in Liberty, and dedicated to the proposition that all men are cre-ated equal.

Now we are engaged in a great civil war, testing whether that nation, or any nation so conceived and so dedicated, can long endure. We are met on a great battle-field of that war. We have come to dedicate a portion of that field, as a final resting place for those who here gave their lives that that nation might live. It is altogether fitting and proper that we should do this.

But, in a larger sense, we cannot dedicate—we cannot consecrate—we cannot hallow—this ground. The brave men, living and dead, who struggled here, have conse-crated it, far above our poor power to add or detract. The world will little note, nor long remember what we say here, but it can never forget what they did here. It is for us the living, rather, to be dedicated here to the unfin-ished work which they who fought here have thus far so nobly advanced. It is rather for us to be here dedicated to the great task remaining before us—that from these hon-ored dead we take increased devotion to that cause for which they gave the last full measure of devotion—that we here highly resolve that these dead shall not have died in vain—that this nation, under God, shall have a new birth of freedom—and that government of the peo-ple, by the people, for the people, shall not perish from the earth.

Before Lincoln's speech most people did not think of the United States as a country "dedicated to the prop-osition that all men are created equal"; after it, it was hard to believe anything less. Lincoln acknowledged the terrible cost in lives of a war he'd conducted, but he assigned that loss significance. He not only gave purpose to the event, he gave meaning to the country itself.

As you think about bad news and how you might fear your people finding out and freaking out, remember Gettysburg. Be it a deal gone bad, a whiffed quarter, or a layoff, this is your chance to define not only the event, but the character of your company. And no matter how badly you screwed up, you didn't send thousands of soldiers to their deaths.

There are companies that don't care about trust. Some leaders foster internal competition. They pit their employees against each other and let the best person win. This dynamic often prevails in businesses where most of the employees have the same function; realms such as venture capital, banking, and "boiler room" sales sweatshops. Because these environments are never collaborative, and often rely on "rank and yank" competitions, there is no internal trust. Everyone says whatever he needs to say to get ahead. Regrettably, this type of dynamic can result in profitable companies.

But I would never want to work there.

Openness to Bad News

If you manage a reasonably large organization, you can be absolutely sure of one thing: at any given moment, something somewhere has gone terribly wrong. Some of your managers know about the brewing disaster, but for reasons we'll get into they haven't told you—even though the mess is only going to grow the longer it stays hidden.

I call these submerged issues *kimchi problems*, because the deeper you bury them, the hotter they get.

How do you build a culture that enables you to discover these problems sooner rather than later? It's surprisingly difficult. There are several reasons employees don't naturally tend to volunteer bad news:

- *It seems to conflict with an ownership culture.* A common management adage is "Don't bring me a problem without bringing me a solution." This idea encourages ownership, empowerment, and responsibility among the employees, but it has a dark side. For one thing, what employees are likely to hear is just "Don't bring me a problem." At a deeper level, what if you know about a problem but you can't solve it? What if you're an engineer who sees a fundamental weakness in your software architecture, but doesn't have the authority or expertise to fix it? What if you're a salesperson who believes one of your colleagues is making fraudulent promises? How can you solve that without help? If you encourage bad news, you must be careful not to disempower people in doing so.

- *The company's long-term goals may not align with an employee's short-term incentives.* Imagine that your new product must ship this quarter. It's so critical you've offered a shipping bonus to the engineers. Now imagine that the product has a dangerous security flaw. If you're an engineer who discovers the flaw, but you need the bonus to buy holiday presents for your children, what do you do?

- *Nobody likes to get yelled at.* If you know about a problem, there's a reasonable chance that you caused it and
  have no idea how to fix it. Revealing it to your superiors means admitting guilt, and who likes to do that?

How do you build a culture that airs its problems without diluting the virtues of ownership and
empowerment—and without making everyone feel defeated, or encouraging a culture of whining?

Encourage Bad News

When I heard about a problem, I tried to seem ecstatic.
I'd say, "Isn't it great we found out about this before it
killed us?" Or, "This is going to make the company so
much stronger once we solve it." People take their cues
from the leader, so if you're okay with bad news, they'll
be okay, too. Good CEOs run toward the pain and the
darkness; eventually they even learn to enjoy it.

Many managers want to attend executive staff meetings, as it makes them feel needed and it puts them in
the know. I made use of this desire by setting a price of
admission to the meeting: you had to fess up to at least
one thing that was "on fire." I'd say, "I know, with great
certainty, that there are things that are completely broken in our company and I want to know what they are.
If you don't know what they are, then you are of no use
to me in this meeting." This technique got me deluged in
bad news, but it also created a culture where surfacing
and discussing problems was not just tolerated, but en-

couraged. We didn't solve all the problems that came up, but at least we knew about most of them.

Sometimes just knowing about a problem we did not solve solved other problems. When I launched Opsware from the ashes of LoudCloud, I wanted to ship Opsware, the software we used to manage our cloud environment, as soon as possible. We would have to scramble to fix the inevitable bugs and issues, but the knowledge and the skills we would gain from competing in the market would be invaluable. That's what I thought.

But most of my engineers thought, Ben has lost his mind. He has no idea how far away this product is from being ready for prime time. I did not know they thought that until, during a routine conversation with one of my engineers, I asked, "What do you think we should do differently?" He said, "Nobody thinks we should ship Opsware but you."

I still thought shipping was right, but I learned that I was creating a different problem: the product team was losing confidence in the CEO. I immediately called an all-company meeting and explained in detail why I thought we were better off trying to sell something that wasn't quite ready and adjusting to market conditions on the fly than waiting until we thought the product was perfect, but not learning anything about our customers' needs in the meantime. I did not convince everyone that I was right, but everyone understood that I was aware of the problems with the strategy and wanted to pursue it nonetheless. That made all the difference.

Focus on Issues, Not People

If you find a problem, do a root-cause analysis and figure out what caused it. You will almost always find that the underlying issue was communication or prioritization or some other soluble problem rather than a particularly lazy or idiotic employee. By getting to the root cause and addressing that, rather than playing the blame game with an employee or two, you create a culture that won't be secretive or defensive—a culture open to bad news.

Look for Bad News in the Regular Course of Business

As you meet with people in your organization, either formally or casually, ask them questions that will help uncover bad news. Questions such as, "Is there anything that's preventing you from getting your job done?" or "If you were me, what would you change in the company?" You may have to ask several times, but people will talk about the problems if you encourage them to. The more you demonstrate genuine eagerness to discover bad news, and genuine supportiveness once it's discovered, the more open they'll be to opening up.

LOYALTY

Loyalty is vital to most cultures—but difficult to install. In today's dynamic business environment, in which the average person can expect to have eleven or twelve different jobs in her career, how loyal are companies going to be to their employees? And how loyal should employees be in return? What are the rewards for each party?

Loyalty emerges from an expectation that the other party feels the same way; that your colleagues, and your company, are there for you. CEOs have different approaches to encouraging it. Here's how Patrick Collison of Stripe thinks about loyalty:

> We obviously can't offer lifetime employment. I hope what we can deliver is that in fifteen years, when people look back, they will think that they were able to do the most meaningful work of their careers here. In exchange, I expect two things: first, ethical integrity. Second, that they optimize for the company rather than for themselves. If they satisfy those two expectations, then they have our appreciation, respect, and loyalty.

In other words, he will support them throughout their careers.

Ali Ghodsi, CEO of Databricks, makes a more specific commitment to his executive staff. "I commit to them that there will be no surprises. The job might not work out, but they will hear that from me first and immediately and they will have time to land safely somewhere else. In exchange, they need to let me know early on if they are unhappy in any way."

Ultimately, loyalty is about the quality of your relationships. People don't leave companies, they leave managers. If there is no relationship between a manager and

244 | WHAT YOU DO IS WHO YOU ARE

an employee or, worse, a bad relationship, you won't get loyalty regardless of your cultural policy. Being explicit in the way Ghodsi is can enhance the relationship, because he makes a verbal commitment on top of the evident interest that he has already taken in his executives. If he simply stated that commitment without working to establish the relationships that would support it, he would fail.

The leader of an organization can have meaningful relationships in the company that extend far beyond the people who report to her. If she takes a genuine interest in the people she meets, stays true to her word, and is known throughout the organization as someone you want to get behind, she can create deep bonds and loyalties even in the most dynamic industries.

YOUR CULTURAL CHECKLIST

With these thoughts on virtues that belong in almost any culture, we've reached the point where you're ready to go make your own. Here's a checklist of points to keep in mind:

- *Cultural design.* Make sure your culture aligns with both your personality and your strategy. Anticipate how it might be weaponized and define it in a way that's unambiguous.
- *Cultural orientation.* An employee's first day at work may not be as indelible as Shaka Senghor's first day out

of quarantine, but it always makes a lasting impression. People learn more about what it takes to succeed in your organization on that day than on any other. Don't let that first impression be wrong or accidental.

- *Shocking rules.* Any rule so surprising it makes people ask "Why do we have this rule?" will reinforce key cultural elements. Think about how you can shock your organization into cultural compliance.
- *Incorporate outside leadership.* Sometimes the culture you need is so far away from the culture you have that you need to get outside help. Rather than trying to move your company to a culture that you don't know well, bring in an old pro from the culture you aspire to have.
- *Object lessons.* What you say means far less than what you do. If you really want to cement a lesson, use an object lesson. It need not be a Sun Tzu–style beheading, but it must be dramatic.
- *Make ethics explicit.* One of the most common and devastating mistakes leaders make is to assume people will "Do the right thing" even when it conflicts with other objectives. Don't leave ethical principles unsaid.
- *Give cultural tenets deep meaning.* Make them stand out from the norm, from the expected. If the ancient samurai had defined politeness the way we define it today, it would have had zero impact on the culture. Because they defined it as the best way to express love and respect, it still shapes Japanese culture today. What do your virtues really mean?
- *Walk the talk.* "Do as I say, not as I do" never works. So

refrain from choosing cultural virtues that you don't practice yourself.

- *Make decisions that demonstrate priorities.* It was not enough for Louverture to say his culture was not about revenge. He had to demonstrate it by forgiving the slave owners.

These techniques will help you shape the culture you want, but remember that a perfect culture is totally unattainable. Your goal is to have the best possible culture for your company, so it stays aimed at its target. If you want people to treat every corporate nickel like it's their own, then having them stay at the Red Roof Inn sends a better cultural signal than having them stay at the Four Seasons—but if you want them to have the confidence to ask for a $5 million order, the opposite might be true. If you don't know what you want, there is no chance that you will get it.

Culture begins with deciding what you value most. Then you must help everyone in your organization practice behaviors that reflect those virtues. If the virtues prove ambiguous or just plain counterproductive, you have to change them. When your culture turns out to lack crucial elements, you have to add them. Finally, you have to pay close attention to your people's behavior, but even closer attention to your own. How is it affecting your culture? Are you being the person you want to be?

This is what it means to create a great culture. This is what it means to be a leader.

AUTHOR'S NOTE

In my discussion of Toussaint Louverture I rely on the following books: *The Black Jacobins: Toussaint Louverture and the San Domingo Revolution*, by C. L. R. James; *Toussaint Louverture: The Story of the Only Successful Slave Revolt in History; A Play in Three Acts*, by C. L. R. James; *This Gilded African: Toussaint L'Ouverture*, by Wanda Parkinson; *The Memoir of General Toussaint Louverture*, translated and edited by Philippe Girard; *Toussaint Louverture: A Revolutionary Life*, by Philippe Girard; *The Slaves Who Defeated Napoleon: Toussaint Louverture and the Haitian War of Independence, 1801–1804*, by Philippe Girard; *Toussaint Louverture: A Black Jacobin in the Age of Revolutions*, by Charles Forsdick and Christian Høgsbjerg; *Bury the Chains: Prophets and Rebels in the Fight to Free an Empire's Slaves*, by Adam Hochschild; and *Tracing War in British Enlightenment and Romantic Culture*, by Gillian Ramsey and Neil Russell.

My thoughts on the samurai have been shaped by *Bushido: The Soul of Japan*, by Inazo Nitobé; *Hagakure: The Secret Wisdom of the Samurai*, by Yamamoto Tsunetomo, translated by Alexander Bennett; *Code of the Samurai: A Modern Translation of the Bushido Shoshinshu of Taira Shigesuke*, translated by Thomas Cleary; *Training the Samurai Mind: A Bushido Sourcebook*, edited and translated by Thomas Cleary; and *The Complete Book of*

Five Rings, by Miyamoto Musashi, edited and translated by Kenji Tokitsu.

Genghis Khan has inspired hundreds of books, and hundreds of viewpoints. I can't say that I have read them all, but I was inspired in particular by *Genghis Khan and the Making of the Modern World*, by Jack Weatherford; *Genghis: Birth of an Empire*, by Conn Iggulden; and *Genghis Khan: His Conquests, His Empire, His Legacy*, by Frank McLynn.

My sense of Robert Noyce and his importance to Silicon Valley owes a debt to Tom Wolfe's article in *Esquire* magazine in December 1983, "The Tinkerings of Robert Noyce," and Leslie Berlin's *The Man Behind the Microchip: Robert Noyce and the Invention of Silicon Valley.*

I quote from my conversations with Shaka Senghor, Reed Hastings, Bill Campbell, Todd McKinnon, Lea Endres, Ralph McDaniels, Mark Cranney, Nasir Jones, Patrick Collison, Michael Ovitz, Larry Page, Stewart Butterfield, Ariel Kelman, Maggie Wilderotter, Don Thompson, Ali Ghodsi, Steve Stoute, and Diane Greene.

ACKNOWLEDGMENTS

There is no way this book would have been written without the constant prodding, everlasting encouragement,
and boundless energy of my darling wife, Felicia. I had
no intention of writing a second book, but she insisted.
For that, and for so many other things, I am eternally
grateful that I met her thirty-three years ago. She is my
inspiration, my muse, my everything.

My friendship with Shaka Senghor was that catalyst
that got me to start writing about a topic I'd long been
thinking about. I am forever appreciative of his generos-
ity in sharing his story and his insights into how culture
works from the ground up.

The conversations I've had over the years with Steve
Stoute have greatly expanded my understanding of culture; his insights on race and inclusion inspired the
chapter on Genghis Khan.

I began the book thinking that I needed to write about
hip-hop culture and how it created the most successful
musical art form of our time. I realized once I got into that
story that I would need an entire book to tell it, but the
inspiration I got from my research proved invaluable to
me as I wrote. Fab 5 Freddy, MC Hammer, Nas, and Ralph
McDaniels were particularly helpful and inspiring.

Bernard Tyson was extremely generous with his time,
especially considering he is running the largest health-
care company in the United States.

I am beholden to Don Thompson, Maggie Wilderotter,

Stewart Butterfield, Todd McKinnon, Mark Cranney, Patrick Collison, Ariel Kelman, Lea Endres, and Michael Ovitz for sharing their stories and insights.

My understanding of Genghis Khan is significantly informed by the work of both Jack Weatherford and Frank McLynn; their books helped me grasp the intimate relationship between Genghis's cultural and military strategies.

I am obliged to Henry Louis Gates Jr. for reviewing the manuscript and helping me make the Toussaint Louverture section as accurate as possible. And I am deeply indebted to Philippe Girard for his amazing research on the Haitian Revolution, which enabled me to begin to frame some thoughts on what set Louverture apart as a cultural thinker.

A number of people read the manuscript and offered incisive suggestions: thank you to Marc Andreessen, Amanda Hesser, David Horowitz, Elissa Horowitz, Felicia Horowitz, Jules Horowitz, Sophia Horowitz, Michael Ovitz, Chris Schroeder, Shaka Senghor, Merrill Stubbs, and Jim Surowiecki.

Thank you to my publisher, Hollis Heimbouch, for encouraging me to write this book. Your belief in me as a writer has been inspiring. And to my agent, Amanda Urban, who gave me the confidence to write about the Haitian Revolution and has been an unparalleled supporter and collaborator.

Finally, I'd like to give a shout out to Tad Friend. Without his help, doggedness, productive combativeness, and commitment to the cause as my collaborator, there would be no book. Thank you, Tad.

Grateful acknowledgment is made for permission to reprint from the following:

"Stillmatic (The Intro)": Words and music by Nasir Jones, Bunny Hull, and Narada Michael Walden. Copyright © 2001 Universal Music-Z Songs, Sun Shining, Inc., WB Music Corp., Cotillion Music Inc., Gratitude Sky Music, and Walden Music, Inc. All Rights for Sun Shining, Inc. administered by Universal Music-Z Songs. All Rights on behalf of Itself Cotillion Music Inc., Gratitude Sky Music, and Walden Music Inc. administered by WB Music Corp. International copyright secured. All rights reserved. Contains elements of "Let Me Be Your Angel" by Bunny Hull and Narada Michael Walden. Reprinted by permission of Hal Leonard LLC and Alfred Music.

"Ready to Die": Words and music by The Notorious B.I.G., Osten Harvey, Sean "P. Diddy" Combs, Barbara Mason, Ralph Middlebrooks, Walter Junie Morrison, Marshall Eugene Jones, Clarence Satchell, and Leroy Bonner. Copyright © 1994 EMI April Music Inc., Justin Combs Publishing Company, Inc., Big Poppa Music, Embassy Music Corporation, Bridgeport Music Inc., and Southfield Music Inc. All rights on behalf of EMI April Music Inc., Justin Combs Publishing Company, Inc., and Big Poppa Music administered by Sony/ATV Music Publishing LLC, 424 Church Street, Suite 1200, Nashville, TN 37219. International copyright secured. All rights reserved. Contains elements of "Yes, I'm Ready" by Barbara Mason. Reprinted by permission of Hal Leonard LLC, Bridgeport Music Inc., and Southfield Music Inc.

"Try Me": Words and music by DeJa Monet Trimble and David Demal Smith Jr. Copyright © 2014 BMG Gold Songs, Lil Loaf Publishing, and DDS 825 Publishing and Copyright Control. All Rights for BMG Gold Songs and Lil Loaf Publishing administered by BMG Rights Management (US) LLC. All rights for DDS 825 Publishing administered by Warner-Tamerlane Publishing Corp. All rights reserved. Used by permission. Reprinted by permission of Hal Leonard LLC and Alfred Music.

"Slippery": Words and music by Joshua Parker, Quavious Keyate Marshall, Kirsnick Khari Ball, Kiari Kendrell Cephus, Radric

permission of Hal Leonard LLC, Alfred Music, and the Administration MP, Inc.

"Honest": Words and music by Nayvadius Wilburn, Leland Wayne, and Gary Hill. Copyright © 2013 IRVING MUSIC, INC., NAYVADIUS MAXIMUS MUSIC, PLUTO MARS MUSIC, and SNRS Productions, WB Music Corp. and Irving Music Inc. All Rights for NAYVADIUS MAXIMUS MUSIC and PLUTO MARS MUSIC administered by IRVING MUSIC. All Rights on behalf of Itself and SNRS Productions administered by WB Music Corp. All rights reserved. Used by permission. Reprinted by permission of Hal Leonard LLC and Alfred Music.

"Wanna Be Cool": Words and music by Sean Anderson, Jeremy Felton, Nathan Fox, Jeff Gitelman, Chancelor Bennett, Nico Segal, Kyle Harvey, Cameron Osteen, Peter Wilkins, and Carter Lang. Copyright © 2015. All rights for CHANCE THE RAPPER administered by CHANCE THE RAPPER LLC UNIVERSAL MUSIC CORP., MY LAST PUBLISHING, OHAJI PUBLISHING, SEVEN PEAKS MUSIC on behalf of Itself, ALL DAY RECESS and THE REAL BRAIN PUBLISHING, SPIRIT ONE MUSIC, JEFF GITTY MUSIC, SONGS OF GLOBAL ENTERTAINMENT, INDIE POP MUSIC administered by KOBALT SONGS MUSIC PUBLISHING, NICO SEGAL administered by PAINTED DESERT MUSIC CORP, CAMERON OSTEEN Publishing Designee on behalf of Itself © 2019 ZUMA TUNA, LLC, WARNER-TAMERLANE PUBLISHING CORP and CARTER LANG PUBLISHING DESIGNEE. All Rights for MY LAST PUBLISHING and OHAJI PUBLISHING administered by UNIVERSAL MUSIC CORP. All Rights for ALL DAY RECESS and THE REAL BRAIN PUBLISHING administered by SEVEN PEAKS MUSIC. All Rights for JEFF GITTY MUSIC and SONGS OF GLOBAL ENTERTAINMENT administered by SPIRIT ONE. All Rights on behalf of Itself and ZUMA TUNA and CARTER LANG PUBLISHING DESIGNEE administered by WARNER-TAMERLANE PUBLISHING CORP. International copyright secured. All rights reserved. Reprinted by permission of Hal Leonard LLC, Alfred Music, and co-publisher(s).

"Gorgeous": Words and music by Malik Jones, Gene Clark, Jim McGuinn, Kanye West, Ernest Wilson, Mike Dean, Scott Mescudi,

Music Clearance Services by Anna Keister of Forza Rights MGMT, LLC.

INDEX

ABOUT THE AUTHOR

Ben Horowitz is a cofounder and general partner at Andreessen Horowitz (a16z), a venture capital firm that invests in entrepreneurs building the next generation of leading technology companies. He is also the author of the *New York Times* bestseller *The Hard Thing About Hard Things*. Prior to a16z, Horowitz was cofounder and CEO of Opsware (formerly LoudCloud), which was acquired by Hewlett-Packard for $1.6 billion in 2007. Horowitz has an MS in computer science from UCLA and a BA in computer science from Columbia University. He lives in the San Francisco Bay Area with his wife and three children.